One Southerner's lighthearted glimpse of the South during the 1940s and '50s in Southern Middle Tennessee and North Alabama.

Loretta Merrell Ekis

1

Dedication

This book is dedicated to the memory of my parents, Fountain Clay Merrell and Dealie Ferguson Merrell, who gave me their love and my Southern heritage,

And to

The memory of my loving husband, R. W. (Bob) Ekis, who taught me to live, love, laugh, and not to take life so seriously.

And to

My children and especially my grandchildren: Sarah, Elizabeth (Beth), Mark, Brian and James, who may think my life very quaint compared to theirs. Indeed that is true! But I hope they will someday be curious enough about their Southern roots to read about the South and its rich history from history books written by those who actually lived during the Civil War and Reconstruction era. A good place to start would be journals and diaries that were written as eye witnesses to a war that did remove slavery in the South, but it also destroyed homes, churches, businesses and the lives of many a Southerner who had no interest in owning slaves but were victims of the times.

Table of Contents

Introduction...

I grew up in Middle Tennessee, and I couldn't be happier that I was born and bred in that part of the country. I love the South with its musical dialects, its fragrant flowers and its broad spectrum of people and places. Even though many make fun of our drawl and our Southern ways, they can never take away the richness and beauty of the South or the strength of its people.

I came into this life during The Great Depression, and I was brought up on the history of the War Between the States—two difficult but different eras for the South. My beginnings were humble as could be expected for that day and time. I was the 6th of seven children. I learned to deal with my older siblings and survive, and to accept that I was no longer the "baby" of the family when my younger sister, Faye, arrived. Life was hard during the depression. My Dad was young and had to work hard to buy land and build a home during that period. We always had plenty food since we grew most of our own, but spending on anything but necessities was almost unheard of for most families.

I can't tell you much about life in the 1930s. Yet I do recall most of the 1940s, the rationing, the black-outs in the evening during WWII, the military airplanes flying overhead with me thinking they might be enemy planes, and the convoys of Army vehicles that passed by our small farm and much more. The 1950s were a very peaceful time except for those whose sons were called into service during the Korean War. Sadly many did not survive that war.

If you grew up in the South, nothing I say in this introduction will be new to you. You know how the un-Civil War destroyed the South, and I'm not speaking of the slavery issue here. My family did not own slaves nor did many who lived in our area of Tennessee. Yet, they all suffered. Sherman wasn't the only one who caused devastation on his march through the South. Union troops invaded the South, often destroying schools, colleges, courthouses along with their contents, and churches. Many Union soldiers took whatever they wanted from farmers and businesses in their path. There were so many atrocities that one never reads about unless you search for journals and diaries of that period. It is a period that most Southerners would rather forget yet it is a large part of who we are. It is also why people from other parts of the country do not understand us or know why we are the way we are. We are never slow to offer our friendship, but until we've had a chance to get acquainted, we may keep you at arm's length to allow you to prove yourself.

Southerners aren't really much different from other people in this country, and our differences are fading fast. That is one reason I've written this book. I offer it as a little "lighthearted" picture of life as it was when I was growing up in the heart of Dixie. The South is and always will be home to me. I am proud of my heritage, and I want others to know there are beautiful people of all faiths and nationalities that make up the South. I'm Southern through and through, and as my nephew, Gary Broadway, says, I'm Southern born and Southern bred and when I die, I'll be Southern dead.

But first, I have a book to write. I hope that no one is offended at the fun I poke at some of our Southern ways. If so, I apologize and ask that you read it with a different mindset…that of looking at some of our traditions and thinking, well, yes, some of them are kind of funny. But that's what gives us our Southern personality and I'm proud of it. I hope you are too.

Casserole Toting Widows and Divorcees

How I Failed This Test

Women are nurturers. It is something we learn from our mothers, aunts and grandmothers. While I tend to think it is a learned trait, it may very well be genetic. In fact, I suspect it is a secret ingredient in mother's milk that is filtered out of male infant feedings. From the time we're toddlers, we understand it is our duty to take care of children and the men folk—which we think of as one and the same. Because of this trait, there are many casserole toting widows and divorcees in the heart of Dixie. Alas, I am not one of them.

As a newspaper writer/reporter/columnist/editor, I often wrote about my foibles and the frequent disasters in my life. After I became a widow, I told my entire reading audience that I didn't cook anymore nor was I about to start. To my dismay, I learned years later that I had set myself up to remain single for the rest of my life. I inadvertently told all the eligible and soon-to-be eligible older men in the readership that I wasn't available. I did it by confirming that I was not a casserole toting widow, and it wasn't likely I would ever join the army of Southern women who were.

It may be indicative to the South, I'm not really sure, but I'm told that some ladies rush to the grocery store, cook their tastiest man-sized casserole, and appear on the doorstep of an unsuspecting widower within days of his wife's funeral. Sometimes, the lady uses chocolate chip cookies to entice the gentleman to notice her, but either way, they are noticed. I often wondered how some women, who were neither very attractive nor smart, managed to marry two, three or more times. In studying the situation, I realized that as soon as an old fellow became single, there was some woman strapping on her apron and getting ready to overwhelm him with her cooking. What did they have that I didn't have? Now I know it wasn't looks or brains. It was a succulent casserole or a plate of cookies.

7

If a man loses his wife, the entire community will rally around him and include him in their family gatherings and outings. The same can't be said for women who become widows. Few invite them to dinner...male or female. No, those holiday invitations are offered to the men who have been left behind by death or divorce. If a married friend learns her best friend has her eyes on a certain gentleman, the two of them will be invited for a dinner party or holiday dinner. That never happened to me. I did have one female friend who cautioned me within weeks of my husband's death that her husband was off limits. She need not have worried. He was already off limits in more ways than one. In fact, ladies, most of you need not worry about someone stealing your husband. If you lose him, however, don't look my way—remember I don't bake.

It was always my belief, and the way I was taught in my youth, that the gentleman always pursued the woman if he wished to form a relationship. Boy! Was I behind the times? While I was busy raising a family, working and taking care of a husband and home, these women became liberated--so liberated, in fact, that they now make the first move in the pursuit of wedded bliss. Instead of waiting for a fellow to call, these ladies were scouting the obituaries and making their grocery lists. When you're 16-25 years old, waiting for a fellow to call is sound logic. That is the proper course of events. However, when you are sliding down the banister of life on a greased cane, that plan no longer works. You join the battle of the cooks, reach out and grab the golden ring (pun intended), or you get left behind in the dust of coattails swishing their way to Old Jim's house with a plate of cookies.

I always thought I was fairly intelligent, but today I look back over the past two decades and realize I wasn't anywhere near as smart as I thought. Had I been, I would have been in the kitchen testing recipes (something I did for Betty Crocker many moons ago) and keeping up with current obits. But I was not smart, so I was left standing with an empty casserole dish in hand while all the eligible men under 95 remarried or attached themselves to some lady who knew how and when to fill that dish.

While I was busy informing people about the events in their cities, towns, or counties via my newspaper job, these ladies were content to stir up a pot of stew and invite over an aging Casanova. It does me no good to cry over a spilled casserole, so I've taken notice of the women men choose. Typically these women are very good at acting and pretending. Men are checked out thoroughly by these women, and when they meet certain specifications, namely money and/or the ability to drive after dark, the lady moves in making him feel as if he is 20 years old. That is something I could never do. My acting skills are zilch. Besides love is blind and I have 20-30 vision--or did at the time. I can't pretend that the little old bald fellow sitting in front of me at church looks like Mel Gibson – uh huh, no way. It isn't that I expect an older person to be a perfect specimen of humanity...it's just that I can't pretend they are. Never was good at pretending. Had we had drama classes in my high school, I would have been assigned to set design or play writing. I was never good at acting.

So, I continue to walk through life alone. It isn't all bad. I have lots of time to read, write, study, enjoy my grandchildren and travel if I wish. I don't even own a pet to keep me tethered to one spot. So, perhaps being alone at this stage of life has some benefits. One of those is that I do not have to answer to anyone about what I wear or how I spend my money. Nor do I have to bake and cook unless I wish. But there might be other advantages to finding an eligible bachelor, so with that in mind I'm going to start test-driving some recipes. Just in case the shadow of some rich, old fellow, who thinks he is Mel Gibson, falls across my path. I've even bought a new mixer and rummaged in my cookbooks to find my best recipes. I've dusted off the stove, and I'm ready to go. Now I have to get busy reading those obits on a regular basis. Also, I must remember not to wear glasses, and I hope he doesn't either.

PVT Robert William Ekis, 101ˢᵗ Airborne, WWII

Note: I was married to a wonderful man, Bob Ekis, with whom I shared 35 happy years. My writing about Casserole Toting Widows and Divorcees is just my way of laughing at myself and continuing to find some humor in life. I have found happiness and contentment in my single state because during this time I've grown stronger in my faith and my walk with the Lord. To paraphrase the Bible, whatever state you find yourself in, therein be content. I am content.

Poke Sallit Time In The Valley...

There was a time if you asked a Southerner for kohlrabi; it might have been interpreted as an insult, resulting in a fat lip or black eye. Kohlrabi could have meant anything to a Southerner from a gentle put down to the equivalent of saying, "Yo mama wears combat boots." We had never heard of some of the more "exotic" vegetables that now grace the tables across the south and the country.

Kohlrabi, bok choy, artichokes, asparagus or any other weird sounding vegetable was not in our vocabulary. In fact, few of us ate iceberg lettuce on a regular basis, and spinach was practically unheard of in our area of the South despite Pop Eye's bulging muscles.

The greens that decked our tables were mustard greens, turnip greens, or collards. The first two were common in our home, but not the latter. Collard greens were prohibited. My Dad didn't like any kind of greens, and my Mama refused to even consider cooking collards. They still smell awful to me. The other two greens were usually available in the spring or late fall, and Southern women cooked and served them with the potliker (for those of you who aren't from the South, potliker in English is pot liquor) -- the juice left in the pan after the greens cooked down—meaning we cook greens and green beans until they are totally dead—never crunchy. The greens were then served with lots of cornbread, green beans, raw onions and fried or mashed potatoes, etc. Of course, we always topped our greens off with either plain apple cider vinegar or pepper vinegar. Either way, the greens were the nectar of the gods, and still are to me. I love them, and would eat them as often as possible if I still lived in the South where they are readily available.

There is another green, however, that still can draw a loud argument even among Southerners, and that is Poke Sallit (or in regular English: poke salad). If I remember correctly, the word sallit comes from the Scots, and apparently made its way to the American South where many Scots settled.

11

There are some of us who love the taste of poke sallit cooked with eggs. Others want nothing to do with the plant we call poke, but whose real name is: Pokeweed, the common name for the plant family Phytolaccaceae, of the order Caryophyllales, and for its representative genus, Phytolacca. We're speaking biologically here since I cannot even pronounce those words. It is also known as American Pokeweed, Cancer-root, Cancer jalap, Inkberry, Pigeon Berry, Pocan, Poke, Poke Root, Pokeberry, Virginian Poke, and Yamilin. But where I grew up, it was called Poke. The berries of the plant are poisonous; we often used them to write our names on cotton sacks. But the plant is also used for medical purposes. So, for those who turn up your nose at poke sallit, pokeweed or whatever name you wish to call it, it is good for you. If you don't believe me, just take a ride on the Internet and look it up. It might surprise you that is has sterling qualities.

In some areas in the South, it is so revered that festivals are built around this nondescript wild plant. The best poke for cooking is the young tender shoots that come up in the spring when the plants are still about 18 inches tall and the leaves less than six inches. If it gets taller than that, don't pick it. It is poisonous. But when it pokes its head above the warming soil, you know it is soon time to pick and cook a mess of greens.

Southern cooks know this weed must be properly cooked. So we cook it twice to remove any poisons in the plant. After the second boiling, Southerners then pour off the liquid and place the greens in a frying pan to which a good amount of bacon grease has been added. Once the greens begin to cook in the fat, stir in a couple of beaten eggs and add salt and pepper to taste. My daddy always said that the more eggs you added, the better, but the purist likes the taste of poke. My dad never liked it and would chide me about eating it. I liked the taste then and still do. As I said earlier, there are many who wouldn't touch poke if they were starving. Others will allow it to be placed on the table and suffer through the smell, but some really love the taste. I am one of the latter. I've always enjoyed a serving of poke sallit, and Mama would always cook some for me whenever I came back home from various parts of the country where I lived.

Eating poke was a springtime ritual in the South, but it is no longer. I suspect you could mention the word to the last several generations of Southerners, and they wouldn't have any idea what it was or if they did, would not recognize the plant growing around the farm. So many of the younger generations moved off the farms, and pokeweed isn't something you look for in cities or towns, though some nice birds planted some in my courtyard here in Kansas City about two years ago. I didn't let it grow because I didn't want anyone trying to eat the berries, but I appreciated them giving me a nice memory. One day, our great-grandchildren will read about their great-grandparents eating poke sallit and head to their computer dictionaries to discover what they were eating. Just look for pokeweed kids. You'll find it. But it is a wild plant that grows in the southern USA, and as I've learned, even as far north as northeast Kansas.

NOTE: For all you non-Southerners please don't eat the poke berries, the mature leaves, the stalk or the root. These could be toxic, and I sure don't want to lose a loyal reader. If you're hungry for greens, perhaps you can do as they do in the North, eat dandelion greens. Lord knows, the South has enough dandelions to feed the armies of several countries. But if dandelions don't appeal to you, there is always kudzu…that fast and fierce growing vine brought over from Japan many years ago. It's about the only thing I know of that may yet defeat the South! It may eventually cover the entire southeast and the ruins will be found in the year 5001 with much speculation how kudzu got here from the orient.

Mama Didn't Believe In Psychology

Today's modern mothers read all the books on how to raise children. They listen to Oprah (who has no children), take classes on child rearing (from professors who have no children) and meet with their contemporaries to discuss how to handle their sometimes willful children. My Mama didn't do any of those things. She had the answer to a stubborn child, of which I was one, and it had nothing to do with psychology. To Mama, discipline was administered on the spot, and it almost always fit the crime.

Having given birth to seven children, Mama wasn't always long on patience. My brothers and sisters and I knew when she had had enough of our shenanigans. Mama had a slight blaze shaped birthmark on her forehead that was barely noticeable unless she got very angry. Most people would never know it was there because she had beautiful olive skin that was a product of what her father called being Black Irish. Black Irish indicates a person with Irish and Spanish blood. The only time I ever saw that blaze was when one of us committed an infraction that made her really angry. Then the red blaze would pop up, and we knew that either she was going to have a stroke or our fannies were going to get stroked. It was always the latter.

We weren't bad kids, but if Mama were alive today she might argue that point. We were just always looking for something to relieve the boredom of growing up in the country and having to entertain ourselves on a hot summer day. My two brothers were more often the bone of Mama's contention, but I confess my sisters and I did our share to awaken the mama bear's roar. To paraphrase Sarah Palin, the difference between a mama and a mama bear is their roar. Mama could almost make you think she was a bear by her own roar. From what my sister Marie tells me, she brought out Mama's roar on a number of occasions. I don't doubt it because I did as well.

Once my brother Tom, who was four years my senior, was having fun shooting his slingshot. Back in the 1940s, kids didn't have many store bought toys, and a slingshot or a whistle made from certain tree limbs provided hours of entertainment. One afternoon Tom and my other brother Clay were trying to see who could hit various targets with their slingshots. The shooting and the bragging went on for quite some time, with each trying to outdo the other.

After a while, Tom turned to Clay and said, "Hey, Clay, I bet I can shoot the eye out of that old hen over there." Clay, the elder of the two, looked back with skepticism on his face and said, "I'll bet you can't." The challenge was on. Tom picked up a small rock, pulled back on his slingshot and let it fly. That poor old hen started flopping around and raising cane, but it was nothing compared to the cane Mama raised.

Clay and I were shocked that Tom actually did hit that old hen's eye, so we just stood and watched her flop as did Tom who was equally shocked. About thirty seconds later, Mama flew out of the house with a broom in her hand and yelled, "What happened to my hen?" Clay and I just stood there saying nothing. Tom, who by this time had pocketed the slingshot, said, "Maybe something hit her."

Mama was sharp as a tack. She knew the culprit and what he had done. With the broom still in hand, she gave Tom's backside a pretty good sweeping that day. Of course, the broom didn't hurt, but he knew he'd better act as if it had. So, he started crying and saying, I didn't mean to hit her. He spent the remainder of the day, walking kind of stiff legged whenever Mama was near so she'd think she had really tanned his hide. But Mama really did get the better of him that day. She confiscated that slingshot and Tom had to take up a new pastime, whittling.

During the war years (WWII) Daddy was away working at Oak Ridge, Tennessee, during the week so it was up to Mama to keep us on the right track. She didn't save everything for Daddy when he arrived home on

Friday night but took care of matters as they arose. She wasn't an overbearing person. She could be as much fun as anyone when we were behaving. It was just that she was constantly having to put out disputes or keeping us from killing ourselves. She had to be swift with justice because she was the only judge in town and her caseloads would have overwhelmed her if she hadn't. If we committed a "crime," justice was there and the scales were always in her favor, I might add.

Judge Roy Moore of Alabama didn't have a thing on my Mama. Mama not only had the 10 commandments, but she added a few to the list where we were concerned—such as, "Thy shalt not maim thy brother or sister." We knew she meant it too, though it didn't stop my brothers from trying to maim me when she was nowhere near. Another rule was "Thy shalt not talk back to your mother." We didn't, but we did a lot of mumbling under our breath out of her earshot.

Another unwritten commandment had to do with the veracity of our statements, such as "Thy shalt not lie to your parents." If you told Mama a white lie and she caught you, that red blaze on her forehead became a neon sign, and she would have you doing penance for not only the commission of lying, but the omission of telling the truth. Now maybe those are one and the same, but I think Mama had her own standard for determining that factor, and we learned to live by it. Lying was not permitted at our house.

I remember, almost too well, one instance when her blaze lit up and would have put a Las Vegas casino sign to shame. I believe it even caused the sun to dim that day. In the 1940s, an old blue bus with three benches running lengthwise of the bus was our transportation to elementary school. As I remember, we called it the Blue Goose. We had to walk down the highway about a quarter mile to catch the bus where it made a U-turn and went to the elementary school at Cash Point. My two brothers, who often led me into trouble, and I hurried out that morning to catch the bus. It was a beautiful spring morning with birds chirping, the sun shining and a day of

17

school was not on our minds. We walked past what would years later be called Slaughter Pen Road and past a small wooded area where the road curved slightly. The bus stop could not be seen from our house.

I don't recall which of my brothers made the suggestion, but I know that one of them did. "Let's hide behind these trees and pretend we've missed the bus." Being a little sheep, I followed them behind the trees. We squatted down so that neither Mama nor the driver could see us. We watched the bus come and go, and then we walked back to the house. We put on a big show about how upset we were that the bus had already run. Mama didn't totally believe us; but she didn't have much choice since she did not drive or have a car at her disposal, and there were no phones at school. I did see that look on her face that said, "You better be telling the truth."

Daddy was at work so we thought we were home free. But nothing was lost on Mama. She made us work around the house and yard all day. To me that was far worse than going to school because I liked school. And I didn't like weeding and picking up sticks and stones from our large yard. I didn't tell Mama that we purposely missed the bus. First of all, I did not want to see her angry, and secondly, my brothers would wreak havoc on my body if I did. I kept my mouth shut and hoped she wouldn't find out.

Right after lunch, a neighbor walked over to our house to visit with Mama. When she saw the three of us there, she asked why we were not in school. Someone told her we had missed the bus. She looked us up and down and said, "I don't know how you managed that. I saw y'all walking to the bus stop a good bit before it run."

Mama didn't let on like she heard, but we knew she had. Sometimes it seemed she let us wait a bit for our punishment. When the neighbor went home, she took us to task and threatened us within an inch of our lives if we ever did that again. She said she wasn't about to raise a bunch of lazy, ignorant, lying kids. We had our own ideas of what that meant, and we (individually and unspoken) decided then and there we were not going to test those waters. We each were chastised and properly disciplined…all without the aid of Dr. Spock. Lesson learned? Don't ever lie to Mama again, and never play hooky from school.

We knew Mama would be hard to live with the rest of the day, and she was. Every time we finished one job, she had six more laid out for us to do. I remember Tom and Clay were set to clearing sassafras bushes from a fence row. By the end of the day, we were dragging; and we were sorry we had not gone to school. Mama made a deep impression on me that day, and the only other time I ever skipped classes at school was once in college. I can tell you that even though I was 19 years old, I didn't enjoy the movie I saw that afternoon. I was guilt ridden. Mama wasn't even in the same town, but I knew she would have made me feel I had somehow committed an "unpardonable" sin. Maybe I did. I just know that I've never "enjoyed" doing things I shouldn't do because I have full knowledge when I am in the wrong. A guilty conscience is hard to live with. If God hadn't put his word in my heart, Mama would have made sure it was there during our youth. Of that I am certain.

No, my Mama didn't use psychology. She used good common sense in dealing with us, and she knew exactly how to mete out punishment according to the crime. When we broke one of her rules, she didn't hesitate to take care of the situation. DHR would probably put Mama in jail today for paddling our rumps, but I can tell you I have never regretted that Mama made us toe the line. She was loving, kind, generous and good to us in many ways, but we knew we had boundaries, and we knew not to cross them. She could be as hard as nails when the occasion called for it, but she was a softy, too. There was never any doubt as to which role she would be playing on any given day or hour—it all depended on our behavior. Our rule of behavior was don't mess with Mama unless you want her messing with you. She applied the same rules to our cousins when they were visiting our home. We all knew she meant business, and on most days we didn't mess with her.

Mama died on April 7, 1991, just one day after her 88th birthday - God bless her soul. She had a difficult earthly life giving birth to and rearing children during the depression years, the war years and losing three of her children before she passed on to eternity. She was a very good mother to all of us, and I know I speak for my siblings when I say we miss her more and more every day. She was indeed a Steel Magnolia in the nicest sense.

Dealie and Fountain (Fount) Merrell – 1940s

Words – Deviled or Dressed

Southerners like words, and we love to tell stories. If you don't believe it, just read the works of Tennessee Williams, Margaret Mitchell, Eudora Welty, Katherine Porter, Lewis Grizzard, and John Grisham to name a few. I'm not in their league, and I'm the first to admit it. But I do enjoy the written language and the talking. I'm sure it is a trait passed down through some Celtic gene and reaches to the depth of my soul.

Southern writing probably gets its story-telling influence from the Scot-Irish who populated the South. Add to that mixture, the romantic French, the staid Germans, the formal Brits, the vibrant Blacks, Creoles, and Cajuns, and you have about all the ingredients needed to fill a library with stories written by Southern writers on a wide range of subjects.

Even our foods show the subtle and not so subtle differences in the backgrounds and cultures that have formed the South. Take eggs for example.

In my family, my mother boiled eggs and then deviled them. To the egg yolks, she added salt, pepper, mayonnaise or Miracle Whip, mustard, vinegar and pickle relish. The egg yolk mixture was fluffy with a tangy-sweet flavor. It was, and still is, one of my favorite foods. Don't ask me what influenced my mother's method of making deviled eggs or the reason they were called deviled. I don't know. I was always too busy eating them to ask dumb questions about origins. Now I wish I had.

I did read somewhere a few years ago that deviled eggs actually originated in Rome. They became popular throughout Europe with the French referring to them as Mimosa, and apparently made their way to this continent when our forbearers came here in the early years. The term deviled eggs probably comes from the mustard and pepper that is used in them. Who knows? I just know they are good!

Not everyone in our community, however, deviled their eggs. Some ladies stuffed their eggs or dressed them. I still find myself stifling a giggle when I hear someone say they had dressed eggs for lunch. I immediately picture a fat little egg sitting on a fence, looking very much like Humpty-Dumpty, or a fat little egg dressed in tie and tails stepping into a limo, penguin style.

I'm not certain how the eggs came to be called dressed unless it was because in taking them to a church function the ladies did not want to bring "deviled eggs' so they referred to them as dressed or stuffed. I do know that within three square miles of where I grew up, there are cooks who dressed, stuffed and deviled their eggs, and they all looked and tasted pretty much the same to me.

Another food that is called by different names is that bread mixture so popular at Thanksgiving. In the South, we refer to the mixture as dressing. No cook worth her Southern heritage "stuffs" a turkey.

Our dressing is mixed and baked in a casserole dish, and it may accompany a turkey, a baking hen or ham. It all depends on what is available at the market. When I was growing up, it was an old hen that was baked alongside the casserole, and yes I do remember seeing the chicken being "slaughtered" the day before it was to be cooked and consumed. That may sound gross to my grandchildren, or even my children, but at least I do understand the saying that someone acts "like a chicken with its head cut off." The chicken does flop around after the head has been removed. This helps to rid the bird of its blood. I'm thinking it does anyway. I've never killed a chicken for dinner, but I know how. I have bought whole chickens and cut them into proper pieces for cooking. There is really nothing to it, but I seldom see whole chickens at the supermarket except in the rotisserie section. Have people completely quit buying whole chickens that are not cooked?

The term stuffing is more often a term found in the North. If you hear the word stuffing used in the South, you can be assured of one thing. Your grandpa didn't settle in the South BEFORE the Civil War. In Southern terms, that would be a transplanted Yankee. I do not mean to insult anyone from outside the South. I would remind you that I married one of those transplanted Yankees, and he loved the South. He was a good man who loved my big, extended family and enjoyed Southern delicacies such as ham, redeye grave and grits. But he did like a "stuffed" turkey, and it wasn't cornbread dressing. I had to learn to cook his beloved Yankee foods, and I did learn good things from him and his Mom—such as New England boiled dinners, corned beef and cabbage and more. There are good cooks in both the North and the South. No one can lay claim to the best cooking. It is all good, but as different as day and night in various sections of the country. I enjoy all types of cooking, but the food I hungered for most when I was out of the South was my Mama's.

What do you call a drink that is made with carbonated water, flavoring, sugar and loads of chemicals? In the land of magnolias and kudzu, we do not call carbonated drinks pop, and often we don't even call them sodas. If you ask a country store clerk where to find a soda, he'll probably send you to the baking aisle in the grocery for bicarbonate of soda. If you ask for pop, he'll say, "Son, I ain't seen your daddy in days."

In my native South, a soft drink as opposed to hard liquor is a coke with a lower case "c." If you're a true-blue Southerner, you don't even use the words soft drink. Every carbonated drink is a coke or co-cola. If you don't believe it, drive up to a small, rural gas station and ask where the co-cola machine is located. Of course, today the word is typically shortened to coke. But if you ask for a coke in the South, you may find yourself drinking an actual Coke, a Pepsi or Dr. Pepper. They all look the same though they have their own followings due to differences in taste.

When I was growing up Daddy ran a sorghum mill during the late summer and fall. It sat down below our house in a wooded area, and the big mill was motor driven and noisy to my ears. However, I loved being in those woods when Daddy was cooking. He had a long sectioned tray built over an "oven" like structure with several compartments that opened to allow the syrup to flow into the next part of the vat when it reached a certain stage. The raw cane juice was poured into a tray at one end and slowly cooked by moving it through the various sections until it came out the other end as beautiful amber sorghum molasses. Daddy was known as one of the best molasses makers in the county, and people from miles around brought their sorghum cane to him for processing and taking home some delicious sorghum molasses at the end of the day.

My favorite thing in the entire world was to take the gallon cans and lids down to the mill so that I could get a treat. Daddy would ladle hot foam from the boiling molasses vat onto a can lid that may have been bent and unusable as seals, and give me a clean piece of sorghum cane whittled like a scoop to dip it with. It was so yummy that I can remember the taste to this day. We never bought molasses because we always had the best made at home. Daddy did this as much to have molasses for the winter as to help out the neighbors. They grew the cane, cut it and brought it to the mill. He took a share of the molasses as payment for his work. It was a good deal for the farmers and our family. Mama used the molasses for baking, and we used them as table syrup as well. Don't ever suggest to me that Black Strap Molasses are the same. They are nothing at all like good Southern sorghum molasses. Black strap molasses are a by-product of sugar cane, and I don't like them. I want the real thing—beautiful amber colored syrup made from sorghum cane.

*****

Fruitcake. Now what can I say about fruit cake that hasn't already been said a million times, and usually in a derogatory manner. I like fruit cake. I love the taste of all the different candied fruits in the small amount of batter. Mama used to make the best, moist fruit cake in the country; and she made one each Christmas. She baked the cake, which must have weighed about 5 or 6 pounds in a ring pan, such as an angel food cake pan, several weeks before Christmas. During those weeks, she would moisten it with grape juice. Others use whiskey or rum depending on what is available. As Christmas rolled around, the cake was removed from its wrappings and joined a host of other desserts made only at Christmas. It was nice and moist. I love a fruit cake that is filled with fruits and nuts. I really don't care if people do make fun of it. If you have a fruit cake that is not good, or one that is hard, toss it out. A good fruit cake is yummy and moist. But until you have savored a homemade fruit cake, you haven't had fruit cake. However, if anyone gives you a Claxton's fruit cake for Christmas some year, I'll be happy to take it off your hands. It's a close copy of my Mama's fruit cake, only not as good. Sorry Claxton's.

*****

Fried foods are common in the South, and we are known for our Southern fried chicken. My Mama made the best fried chicken. I can remember when she would go out into the chicken pen and chose a fat little hen for Sunday dinner. She always selected the chicken and wrung its neck or chopped off the head herself. The chicken was then allowed to dance around until it fell over dead. In doing this, most of the blood was removed from the body. After it was dead, Mama scalded the entire chicken and plucked the feathers. Its innards were removed, along with the feet and head. Then it was thoroughly washed, and placed it in a covered bowl to refrigerate. Before cooking, she marinated it for at least 30 minutes or longer in buttermilk.

Buttermilk made the chicken moist and tender when cooked. After marinating she removed the chicken, and coated it with seasoned flour before placing it in hot oil in a large iron skillet. Pan fried chicken is still the best you can find anywhere, and if you cook it with the bones in, rather than the plain chicken breasts most people buy today, you have a much tastier chicken. I don't know exactly what the bones add to the cooked chicken, but it is a flavor that you don't get with boneless chicken.

When my stepdaughter was married in Washington State many years ago, her new husband's parents, Mr. and Mrs. Medbury, native New Yorkers, came to the Pacific Northwest for the wedding. After the wedding, they came to our house to see the bride and groom off on their honeymoon, and I ended up cooking their dinner. I was not expecting to prepare dinner for company, and I didn't have anything in the house to cook except chicken. So they were treated to Southern Fried Chicken. They went away licking their lips and saying they knew that since I was from the South I knew how to cook chicken. They were right...I did and still know how to fry chicken though I seldom do anymore. Doctors are always taking away the good tasting foods that we all love turning our golden years into dieting years.

My favorite fried food other than chicken is potatoes...no, not French fries. Those are just not the same as good pan fried potatoes. There is nothing better than potatoes fried in a big iron skillet. Today, so few women cook the way our mothers did, in the South or elsewhere. We rely on packaged food to the point that we are destroying our bodies. At least, that is what my cardiologist tells me, and I have to believe he is probably correct. He has suggested to me that I eat foods more in their natural state such as did my hunter/gatherer forbearers. I've been trying, but the funny thing is that people keep running me out of their gardens and orchards. So much for his prescription on diets!

I suppose that means no more fried potatoes, no creamed potatoes, no macaroni and cheese, no chicken and dressing, and no desserts. In other words, I'm going to have to spend the next 15-20 years eating healthy unadulterated foods so that I can live longer in the nursing home. Ah...I knew there was something about this I did not like...living longer in a nursing home where I'll be served mush without any flavoring or seasoning because I won't have any teeth. I suspected there was a catch to his suggestion.

Of course, I'm only poking fun at myself. I will try to stay as healthy as possible in order not to be a burden to my family. But if I want a good fried chicken, then that is what I shall have…in moderation!

*****

During the war years, Mama often made butter rolls. This is such a delectable dessert that I cannot adequately describe it, nor can I make it as my Mama did. She made dough, similar to biscuit dough, rolled it out (not real thin), cut it into squares, and filled the squares with butter, cinnamon and sugar, sealed them and placed them into a baking pan. I always remembered her adding water to the pan, but my older sister said she added milk and baked the rolls…possibly added some vanilla too, I don't recall. All I remember is that when they came out of the oven piping hot, we feasted on manna from heaven. It is a simple dessert for the family, but a delicious one. It seems to me that she often sprinkled a little nutmeg on top before baking them, but I can't really recall. If anyone has the recipe for this simple dessert, I'd love to have it.

*****

Iced tea is common across the United States, but in most places it is served unsweetened, and if you prefer it sweet, you have to ask for sugar or sweetener. I can only say one thing about unsweetened tea, it is not good. The only tea that I like is so typically southern that I've had difficulty finding it in other places, and believe me, I've tried. I like my tea sweetened while it is still warm, so that the sugar is dispersed through the tea and no grainy effects left. I've argued with people that it is different than sweetening tea that is ice cold. If you stir sugar into a glass of iced tea, it does not taste the same.

Of course, I am rather fanatical about what brand of tea I use. It has to be the black pekoe tea packaged in Louisiana. It must be properly steeped, sweetened when still warm, and served over ice with a big slice of lemon. That to me is the only "soft" drink that is worth drinking on a hot summer day. It is a real thirst quencher.

*****

My parents grew a huge garden every year even into their 80s, and believe me I've spent many a hot hour planting cabbage and onions, sticking pole beans, picking tomatoes, picking up potatoes, and shucking corn. I love almost all vegetables, but I do not like some of the cool weather vegetables such as kale. Fortunately, that was not a vegetable grown in the South when I was young, so I never ate any. When I did finally try kale a few years ago, it almost made me gag. Now I can understand why Yankees think turnip greens taste so bad. You eat what you're use to when you are growing up, and kale wasn't one of those things. We seem to develop taste buds according to what we eat when we are young. For instance, I love cooked turnips. My husband liked cooked rutabagas. I claimed that rutabagas tasted bitter to me, and he who was raised eating rutabagas said turnips tasted bitter to him Solution? I cooked turnips for me and rutabagas for him, but not on the same day.

One thing I really miss is having vegetables fresh out of the garden. If you buy your vegetables from a grocery store, they are not as fresh and good as something that you picked and cooked the same day. Nothing compares to corn fresh out of the garden. Cooking it while it is still very fresh retains the sweetness that will turn to starch if not used fairly soon after picking. Another vegetable that is only good fresh off the vine is a tomato. I love a good vine ripened tomato, and I don't want one that has a green taste to it. If it isn't all red, then I don't want it. The same goes for fruit off the tree or vine. We grew up with all our fruits and vegetables coming straight out of the garden, orchard or vineyard. If I could change anything in this life, it would be having access to all those fresh, homegrown products again. Alas, I do not; nor do many who may read this. The best we can do is buy fruits and vegetables from local farmers, farmers' markets or search supermarkets for the freshest and best.

Big Hair, Dress Styles and Beauty Pageants

There are people who think that anyone with big hair is from the South. While that may have been true at some point in time, it isn't necessarily true today. Yes, there are women who still tease (rat??) their hair to make it look like a squirrel's nest, but I've seen them in every part of the country. The South may have its debutantes, but big hair isn't necessarily Southern. Actually, I think big hair must have originated by mating a porcupine with a llama. But then, I've never had big hair so how would I know?

However, I've often wondered why women go to the extremes with hair styles? It must be something to do with our hormones. Women with big hair may be infected with the same strain of hormones that makes a male peacock spread its tail to attract the female peacock. Or it may be that when the hormones begin to diminish in their 30s, the need to call attention to themselves increases. Whatever it is, it is disconcerting when you are sitting in church and can't concentrate on the sermon for wondering if the head of hair in front of you might have mice leaping out onto your lap at any moment. I actually saw such hair here (in the Midwest) at one church service, and it was all I could do to focus on the sermon. Seriously, big hair sometimes looks like something I might pull out of a rag bag to dust my furniture -- if I could stand to touch it, which I can't.

Ladies, let the big hair go. If you want to attract a man, cook a casserole and set it on top of your head. The wafting scent of a good beef stroganoff would bring the man to his knees, and then you can toss him over your back and carry him home with you. If the casserole idea doesn't work, simply pull on some camouflage clothing and sit in a deer blind with your hubby or boyfriend. Just don't take a gun unless you're capable of using it, and I don't mean capable of using it on the man in the blind.

Remember back in the 70s when the hippy movement was in full swing. Long straight hair was all the rage from coast to coast. I think beauty shops must have lost a fortune during the 70s because I don't remember seeing anyone with hair that looked as if it was salon cut. As I recall, the dirtier it was the better the hippies liked it. Today, that same look is in vogue, but at least the hair looks clean today and properly cut. Girls wear their hair scrunched with gel to make it look wet and stringy, or spike it if it is short. Others tie it up in a ponytail, 1950s style, and others get it clipped so short you can't tell if they are a boy or girl unless you see they are wearing bras under their shirts. Even that might not be a clue as to the sex.

I remember in the 1950s when the ladies in my home town trekked to the beauty shop every Friday or Saturday to get their hair, shampooed and lacquered. That is not a typing error. I worked as a telephone operator for my Dad during my high school years, and I was right next door to Blondie's Beauty Shop, which many of the ladies frequented. These women would come to the beauty shop with their hair piled high on top of their heads, go through the washing, rolling and drying process, and come out looking exactly the same as they did when they went in. They had so much lacquer on their hair that if you touched it, it probably would break. I hope they stayed away from cigarettes until it thoroughly dried. I could not see much point in their "dos." I remember one woman with jet black hair, no doubt a dye job, wearing her hair in a beehive hairdo, and it looked weird even then.

Remember machine perms? In the 1950s, I was the "victim" of a "machine" perm. Your hair was placed on rollers that were connected to a machine that would heat them when it was turned on. I always came out looking as if I had stuck my finger in an electric socket and received a shock that curled my hair. I hated those perms, but they were the rage in the 40s and very early 50s. After that came cold wave perms, similar to the Toni's and other brand named perms on the market then. Perms have always frizzed my hair, so today I wear it straight.

I don't like a hairdo that looks the same week after week, and I don't like one where I have to go to the beauty shop on a weekly basis and have it set, trimmed, moussed or gelled. I prefer hair that can be washed daily and requires little time to maintain. I can't even imagine going a full week without washing my hair, but I am sure many still do. I just hope they don't have mice nesting in their hair or worse.

One thing that always amuses me is how many women who are natural brunettes bleach their hair blond. For the most part, I think God gave us the color hair that goes best with our skin tone and eyes. I love to see a girl with dark hair embrace her look rather than trying to turn into another Marilyn Monroe, Lady Gaga or Madonna. To me the natural look with both makeup and hair color is preferable. I'm not a beauty, and no amount of makeup or hair color is going to change that. But then God never promised me blond hair. Just gray hair as I age. It seems to me almost 99 percent of the women on TV now have blond hair. I think they all must go to the same "TV personality finishing school." They all look alike, dress alike and sound alike. I like variety, so I wish they would stop cookie cutting every woman on TV.

I have had hairdressers who were astonishingly good, and I've had some that were equally as bad. I had a perm in Wichita, KS once that sent me into hiding for about a month. Since my hair is fine, it burned easily, but it wasn't the fault of the solution that time, except for the fact it was left on so long. I was in a department store beauty shop when it happened. The operator had me sitting in a chair waiting for the solution to do its thing when she apparently became angry at someone or something and left the store. Everyone kept working around me, and after sitting there a good five or 10 minutes over the maximum time for the solution to work, I started asking for her. Someone, after another 10 minutes, came and said she had left for the day. They did rinse my hair, but it was so burned I couldn't venture far from the house. I can tell you that nothing much can be done with chemically burned fine hair except to pray that it grows fast.

Another hairdresser used detergent on my hair to strip out hairspray and other gunk that was on it, and then would tell me I needed a conditioner. Well, duh! I would assume so when detergent has just stripped out all the natural oils from the hair. I never complained, but I did know what she was up to and let her get away with it a few times.

*****

Hair styles and dress styles come and go. It is amusing to live as long as I have and see some of the styles of the 1950s come back and be accepted by the young. For instance, Capri pants. Remember when we wore them in the '50s and '60s? Now everyone is wearing Capri pants, young and old. Sheath dresses have also returned and that is a style that I loved in my youth but find no longer so "cute" with no waistline to define…or perhaps for me it is a "waste" line that is defined. Much waste has collected there through the years.

Remember the mini skirt and songs like *These Boots Were Made for Walking?* Goodness, we went from skirts at our ankles to miniskirts that barely covered the bottom seemingly overnight. Women were liberated and they wanted to show off their gams. Not I. I did wear my skirt length just above the knee at one time, but no higher. The very young looked OK in a mini skirt as long as they were slender, but the ultimate in ugly has to be when a grown woman wore the mini with fat thighs gracing every step. For the young movie stars, it might have been a good look, but for women over 35, the look lost a lot in translation. Today, I see the same thing happening again…fat thighs that would be best covered and knees that beg for less exposure. I also see muffin tops…that's where the fat between the lower part of the bra and the upper edge of the pants form a muffin. Ugly is the word. In this case, if you have it flaunt it, isn't good advice. If you have a muffin midsection, cover it. Believe me, I know the look, and it isn't pretty. In fact, I'm trying to find ways to cover my muffin, but no success as yet. Perhaps a diet?

*****

Beauty pageants are not bad in themselves, and I've known young women who were able to go on to college after winning their state's crown. I served a term on the Miss Kansas pageant board that was part of the Miss America contest back in the late 1970s, so I am aware of the benefits. However, I find it abhorrent to see toddlers dressed like strippers. When mothers dress their little girls in frocks that even an adult shouldn't wear, she should be forced to get out on the street and sell her own wares—not the child's, the mother's. If you're going to put your little girl in a beauty pageant, let her natural beauty shine through. Sure, it is OK to have her hair done and even a little lip gloss is not out of the ordinary, but please don't dress them as if they are appearing on a stage in Las Vegas, or worse at the cat houses around Reno. Not everything that is legal is food for the soul or for your child.

When I see little children appearing in the beauty contests on TV, I cringe. Some of those little girls look as if they are 30 years old with their false eyelashes, mini-skirts, and feather boas. Let your little girl live as a child as long as she can. One day, she'll be forced to grow up and her childhood will be gone. Allow her to enjoy her youth without all the fake lashes, makeup and glitzy clothing. I have no objection to girls playing dress-up or appearing in beauty pageants, but dress them age appropriate. Your little girl is beautiful in her natural state. Let her stay that way.

Y'all Come Back, You Hear?

The Southern Expression that seems to cause the most consternation among visitors from other parts of the country is this one: "Y'all Come Back, you hear?" It is simple enough for any grits fed Southerner to understand, so we are often confounded when others don't.

A friend of mine upon moving to the Elkmont, AL area from Milwaukee, WI, said that when she heard this the first time she turned and started back inside the home she had just left. She thought the hostess wanted her to stay longer. When my friend, Pat, expressed this to me, I doubled over laughing. Of course, by then she had figured it out herself and was laughing along with me. "Y'all Come Back" is our way of saying; we want you to visit again soon. To her, it meant, the hostess was asking her to come back into the house right then. No wonder some folks from other parts of the country never know when to leave! And here we thought they were just enjoying our company.

Newcomers to the South should be aware there is as much difference in Southern and Yankee English as there is between British and American English. Southerners, by and large, do talk a bit slower than people in the north, but this is not a sign of laziness but of heritage. However, do not be surprised to hear those who can and do speak at the speed of sound. It is this type speech that is most difficult to understand since the words often run together quickly, syllables are dropped and endings slurred. Just remember if someone asks, "Did je eat yet?" they are asking if you've eaten. If not, they will invite you to join them. We are always generous hostesses.

Another thing to remember is that people in Middle Tennessee do not speak the same as those in East Tennessee or even West Tennessee. We especially don't speak like the people in the Delta area of the South. We don't understand them either. We do know there is an "R" in Mother (not Muhtha) for instance. One difference is the word pecan. Some say pee can while the rest of us say puh-con (or a facsimile thereof). There are huge differences in the speech patterns in different areas of the south. Another word that we don't all agree on is the word caramel. I say care-a-mul…a soft c not a k sound, and I don't shorten the word to sound like karmul. But I won't fight with you over how you pronounce it, as long as you allow me to say it the way I do. Another word is pajama. I say pa-jum-mas while others say pa-jam-mas. I also say toe-ma-toe not toe-mah-toe. We all have our little quirks of speech. No need to call the whole thing off, as the song suggests.

For instance, the people in New Orleans with their mixture of French, Spanish and other nationalities not only sound different; they use different words in many cases to express themselves. The word bayou would be used for the word creek. In Middle Tennessee where I grew up a creek is a creek...not a crick. You'll hear the word "crick" pronounced in places like West Virginia, and Pennsylvania where my husband grew up but not in my home area. If you hear a Southerner using the word crick instead of creek, he/she may come from a different area. Also, if a person calls a canoe a pirogue (pronounced pee row), you know they are from the marshland of Louisiana not Middle Tennessee. Southerners have such diverse backgrounds that it really upsets me to hear people refer to us all as rednecks and say we are uneducated. I know a lot of people with college degrees that often revert back to their Southern speech habits when they are "out of the office." There isn't anything wrong with that, but it seems to give Hollywood great relish to make everyone appear ignorant and slow. Shame on them! It's their loss and our gain, I suppose. We just have to overlook their ill-informed thinking.

So to you, who are new to the South, be aware that the South is diverse. We don't like being lumped together. It would be like saying all automobiles are Chevrolets. We come from different backgrounds, depending on the area in which our forefathers settled. We do have many characteristics that are similar, but we are definitely not all cut from the same cloth.

Even though we are different in many ways, there is a certain spirit that holds together almost all Southern-born. It is called football. We are loyal to our fellow Southerner, unless they happen to cheer for the wrong school, then as my Mama would have said, "It's Katie bar the door," meaning look out, the fur is about to fly (another Southern expression). Sports in the

South are right up there next to the Bible in importance, and sometimes I think sports have topped the Bible in importance. We all have a particular college team, usually depending on which school we or one of our relatives attended, and only an act of God would make us root for the opposing team. Here in Kansas, I see that same culture clash between Kansans and Missourians when the two state universities played one another when they were in the same conference. This competition is often referred to as the Border War…a reference to the Civil War.

I have been amused at how fanatic or rabid some sports fans are. Let a team fall behind the opposing team and fans of the losing team almost foam at the mouth. They make all manner of ugly comments about the coach, the players and especially the refs of the opposing team. I don't know if any studies have been done on how often fights within a family occur over a difference in ball teams, but I'll bet its right up there with the Hatfields and McCoys. Football not only fills stadiums, but it unleashes more fights than guys fighting over a woman at a local bar. Every weekend you'll find fans of all the larger colleges rooting for their teams. I don't think people in the South are more obsessed with football and their favorite team than any other fan, but I think it has become a necessity for many. It is kind of like going to church on Sunday. You just know you have to be there. Of course, if you can't make the game, the next best thing is to watch it on a big screen TV preferably with about 20 others. Cheering is mandatory when your team is winning, but swearing is sometimes an option when the other team is scrambling your team's brains and frying them in motor oil.

We Southerners do love our football, and we'll defend our teams until our dying day as long as they are winning. When our team starts losing, we become highly annoyed and the cheering stops. We call for the coaches to resign, the quarterback to be changed or the powers to be to look into the opposing team that beats us every week to make sure they aren't cheating. It isn't that we don't love our football coaches and players, we do. We just don't like for them to lose. Every state has its own big rival within the state. But in Alabama it is the civil war all over again when Alabama plays Auburn. Then there is Kentucky and Tennessee or Tennessee and Alabama. When those teams kick off, you can hear the Rebel yells starting.

Then not only do good men fuss, fume and curse and sometimes cry like babies; but you may hear some of those saintly women who sit in the pew on Sunday raving and ranting. Of course, we do have something that the north doesn't have. We can yell at our coaches until our hearts are content and call them names as long as we precede it with, bless their heart. Such as bless his heart, that coach is a knucklehead.

Yes, football is sacred in the South, and God help the coach who doesn't win at least 90 percent of his games. If he doesn't live up to his fan's expectations, then he doesn't last as long as a pan of dog food in the cage of a red bone hounds. He's history--without fanfare--without a 'don't let the door hit your rear on the way out,' but with a collective sigh of relief from the fans. Football really is a necessity. For the most part, it keeps us from actually killing one another because we sit on opposite sides of the field. If we didn't have football, we might have more Hatfield and McCoy skirmishes, and that would not be a good, productive way to spend Saturday afternoons or nights.

For those of us born and raised in the South, we wear our Southern heritage proudly and will defend it to the end. Being born in the South means a lot to us. I count it a privilege to have been born and raised in the Tennessee Valley, and I often told my parents after living on both coasts and various places in between that I was happy I was raised in the south. There is no place like home. I'm really proud to be a Tennessean. Though I'm from Tennessee, I am an avid Alabama football fan; but I do not let that get in the way of my relationship with friends who root for other teams. Though we may scream and yell for our teams, when we meet each other on the street, we put the game behind us and act as friends should. We just don't mention the friend's team lost to our team at our next meeting. That would definitely be uncouth, and we don't like being uncouth. Well, OK. There are some people who do, and they like to "rub it in." I just wish we could put aside our differences and remain friends when it comes to politics. Honest debate is always healthy, and not everyone roots for the same team on the field or in politics.

Honeysuckles, Spanish moss, magnolias, soft gentle breezes, hickory wood smoke emanating from someone's fireplace or BBQ grill are things that I associate with the South. When I fly into Huntsville, AL, I love to see fields of cotton growing lush and green in the red dirt of Madison County. Even though I don't want to pick cotton, I still love the smell of raw cotton that has not been tampered with by man or machines.

Those of us who have reached our "golden years" realize that nothing ever stays the same. Just in the Tennessee Valley, we've seen cotton fields give way to suburbs or subdivisions, the bullet factory at Redstone Arsenal of the WWII era give way to missiles, rockets and to the giant Saturn V and the Space Station. We've seen country music and gospel music take a back seat to pop rock and front porches turned into backyard patios so that people can have their privacy. We've seen the cotton mills and their mill villages disappear from view along with cotton gins and other relics of the 1950s.

Another thing we have seen change is the ability for Blacks to live and work alongside us in towns and in the countryside. We've seen separate schools, water fountains and bathrooms become communal. Those are changes that needed to happen, and I don't hear anyone in the South complaining about it. I do hear people in the South even 50 years later complaining that people came from the North to make sure these changes happened on their time, and that is something we Southerners resent— outsiders assuming we don't know what to do and must tell us when and how to do it. Southerners believe in sweeping around your own door stop before cleaning around your neighbor's. Many of the families had good relationships with Blacks in the area and still do, and I firmly believe that things would have changed without bussing people in from the North where Blacks were treated sometimes far worse than they were in the South. Some people in the North deny that Blacks were ill-treated in their areas. They were, and if you look at the Black communities in some of our cities today, they still are very segregated, have poor schools and little chance from escaping their situations. That needs to change, but it will take a huge shift in the culture that holds them there. I hope it will change soon for their good. We are all God's children.

Yes, the South is changing, along with the rest of the homogenized country. But all I can say is that by the Grace of God I'm Southern and proud of it. So Y'all Come back, you hear? But please, don't try to change us. We like who we are.

Number Please...

When I was growing up, we still had telephone operators who answered the calls and connected the caller to another party or long distance. During high school on the weekends and summers, I worked as an operator.

There was nothing fun about sitting at a switchboard and answering calls all day every weekend and during summer vacations, but I did it. Daddy thought it would be good for me, and it was a way to earn money. It also allowed me to sit and read between calls which was all I wanted to do anyway. In rural Lincoln County, Tennessee, there wasn't much to do in the summer except garden, pick cotton, go to a movie, roller skate, or read books. So working was normal for me since movies and roller skating was limited to the weekends only.

I would arrive at 7 a.m. to relieve the night operator, and work until 4 p.m. Of course, there was a lunch break in between. Daddy never minced words about what he expected of me as an employee. I was to set an example for everyone who worked there, and the #1 rule was that I was never to divulge anything said over the phone between two parties.

It was a small town by any standards, and we had fewer than 150 telephones to answer, but it did keep me busy at times. Back then, we had party lines, and people on these lines could and sometimes did listen to other people's calls. In order words, having a phone was the best way to get all the gossip around the area, and believe me many did. Being an operator meant you probably heard it all, too. I did. I knew who was drunk, who was running around on their spouse or boy/girl-friend and much more. But I never talked. Though the average customer did not know it, we had a silencer key that we used to check and see if anyone was still on the line. We were allowed to go in and check, then get back off the line. When the people were finished talking, we disconnected the two lines so that others could use them. I'm telling you officially what we were supposed to do. It didn't always work out that way.

43

One operator was always listening to conversations, and it caused her a bit of a problem, as well as my Dad. We had two or three doctors in town at that time, but one of them notoriously did not like to work on certain days of the week. On those days, he shut down his practice and took a day off, which I'm sure he needed since he made house calls as well as held office hours.

On his days off, his wife would answer the home phone and tell the person calling that he was out on a call and she didn't know when he would be back. Well, as it happens, this one operator was listening to the good doctor planning a fishing date with another fellow in town, and she didn't like the fact the wife was not being honest. So, she tells the next party who called the doctor that he wasn't at home and where he had gone fishing.

Of course, the doctor found out, and called my dad to complain. I don't think I've ever seen my dad angrier than he was with this operator. He told her the next time she told anything she heard over the switchboard she was fired. She shaped up, and I never heard of her spilling the beans again.

Being fairly mature for my age, I knew not to tell anyone things I heard over the switchboard, but I did hear a lot. In all honesty, when I got bored, I listened to conversations. Most were just idle chitchat, but some could have been damaging had they been spread about. I knew which husbands were calling which wives, and they weren't always couples. I also knew when all the teens in town were planning a party and where they were going to hold it—even who was bringing the booze. I even knew when some kids in high school had a drunken spree and the parents were anxiously looking for them early the next morning. Nothing much passed by the ears of an operator in a small town. To this day, however, I've never told anyone what I heard over the switchboard, and should you ask me today, I wouldn't tell you who any of the players were. Some things need to be private.

If you never had a phone when there were still operators and party lines, you have missed some fun times...like trying to sneak a call so that no one would know you were on the party line, but failing. Having people pick up the phone and ring it in your ear while you were holding for another party, or having little old ladies get on the phone and call everyone in the book until they found someone with whom to talk.

I remember one little lady, a distant relative of mine, who was the most talkative little person I have ever known. She would get on the phone and ring and ring and ring for what seemed like five minutes. As an operator, I could not answer the call as long as she was turning the crank on her old wall phone, so I had to wait for her to stop. Then when I did answer, this sweet lady would engage me in conversation for as long as I would let her before putting through her call. She was always so loving and pleasant that I would never have been rude to her, but it was really hard as a teen to make conversation with someone who was 50-60 years older than me. However, I did try. I remember seeing her death notice years after I had married and moved away from home, and thinking that I was happy she had a telephone in her later years. I'm sure it helped to alleviate some of the loneliness of being left alone.

I also knew some men in town who were cads. That is the nicest words I can use to describe them. It seemed that they could not stand for anyone to have a successful business in Ardmore except themselves. They were always giving Daddy a difficult time about their phone service, and even though he was my Dad, I can honestly say that he worked hard at keeping the system operating well. As soon as he could, he built a better system with dial service. I am proud of what he did for my hometown, but I know three men who did not wish him well. I won't name them since some of them have descendants still living in the area, but they were never on top of my "Man of the Year" list. Of course, there were many others who did support my dad, and to them I will always be grateful. The Mims brothers and Mr. Charlie Berry come to mind, but there were others.

Every small town has those who seek power, and they don't want anyone else to interfere with their climb up the ladder. They want to be the big fish in a little puddle, and they will walk over anyone who gets in their way. My hometown was no exception, and I suspect it is still about the same just with different key players today.

One thing my dad always did for the city and town was to string all the Christmas lights every year that he was in business there. That also meant having to take them down. Do you know that until the day he died, he was never given any recognition for this yearly job that took hours of his time, nor did anyone ever thank him? It was just always understood that he would do it, year after year. He did, but it would have been nice had someone said thank you for his efforts and those of his employees who also helped, such as my brothers, Clay and Thomas, and Howard Connor and Carl Whitsett.

My Dad never became one of the political insiders in town--partly because he played by the rules, and partly because he didn't let those who tried, run his business. He was his own man, not a follower; and I'm proud of him for that. He was honest and had integrity, something that didn't always sit well with those who liked to control things.

It was the "controllers" that caused my Dad to get out of business when he did. He was simply tired of fighting "city hall" every step of the way. I use "city hall" simply to indicate those who wanted power and control, not necessarily the heads of the city. He was the first president of the phone company in my home town, and he had the dial system installed and ready to cut over from the old system to the new when he decided to retire. If you were not one of the "in crowd" in town, you were given no credit for anything. It was as simple as that. It is a shame that this still happens in small towns—large ones as well, I'm sure. I am not bitter about these people, but I am writing this to set the record straight as to why my Dad chose not to be a business man any longer in the state line town. When you put in 70 hour weeks on a job, the crabbing on your time off gets old, and they did crab over and over again. I remember it well because I worked there during that time.

Those who gave him problems were few, but annoying enough to make life difficult. Everyone involved during those days is now deceased. I suppose some of them are still striving for power in the afterlife, but that is now their problem.

Today everyone has a cellular phone in addition to land lines. When I was growing up, our first telephone was an old wall-mounted phone with a heavy, chunky receiver, separate mouth piece, and hand crank. You had to stand to use this phone. It was in the living room, and there were no private conversations from boy-friends to be had. Later, we had a wall phone that had a rotary dial on it. My folks had that wall mounted phone as long as they lived. I managed to put in a touch tone phone in their living room and bedroom before they passed away, but my Mother always had difficulty using the phone until I put in auto-dial numbers for her. She loved the convenience of having a phone near at hand in her last years so that she didn't have to run to another room and stand to talk. So much changed during their lives...from horse and buggy days to the space age programs that I wonder how they took it all in. Life never stands still, and we have to ride the waves of change. I cannot begin to imagine what they would think of the changes in this day and age, and I'm grateful that they do not know about many of them.

Telephones are now as much nuisance as a benefit. When I'm walking through a store and hear someone speak directly behind me, I often turn to respond to a question only to realize that they are yakking with a friend about nothing. Can't those calls wait until they are in a private place? I really don't want to know what Mable is wearing to church on Sunday or what John is doing at the tavern until it closes. I'm not interested in the details of their life. Worse still, I don't want you texting while driving. It isn't safe, and I hope that anyone who does text while driving stops before they end up killing themselves and other people. Texting and driving is happening all over the country with sometimes fatal results. Please stop before you end up in a morgue alongside the person you either hit or ran off the road. Involuntary manslaughter is not something you want on your record either.

If I could turn back the clock to a time with less stress and angst, I probably would even if it meant having to shift gears on my car, do without a cell phone as I travel across the country (which I often did before the old bag car phones came into being), and even forego air conditioning in my car. We all survived hot, sweaty cars, shifting gears and not communicating with the world from the drivers' seat. I think it might be fun to put today's youth in these situations and see how they fare. (Uh oh, I hear a lot of groaning from my grandchildren who think I was born the year George Washington was president.) I would imagine they wouldn't be happy, but at the time we didn't know any difference. I do believe that people seemed happier in the 1950s than they do today, but perhaps I was living in a time-warp and didn't realize it. At any rate, I'm happy to have had all the experiences I had through life, especially the chance to say "Number Please," and the chance to pull the plug on a conversation if it went over long. Yes, I did that too occasionally. No one is perfect.

Ardmore Telephone Company In Service Since the 1920s

(Originally Published in Your Community Shopper and written
by *Loretta Merrell Ekis)*

Telephone service in Ardmore may have originated in a store owned by Lonnie Ivy at the corner of what is now Highway 53 (old Stateline Road) and 3rd Avenue on the Alabama side. Velma Parker, a retired school teacher, remembers a phone being in the store building about 1908. She also believes Ivy operated a phone system from his store for a handful of people. This is possible, but there is no actual evidence of this. The area was sparsely settled at that time. The railroad did not come through Ardmore until 1910-11 time frame.

Most old timers, however, recall that Tommy White established the telephone company in Ardmore in the 1920s. Mr. White operated the phone company until his death in 1935. The company was then purchased by his son Haney White. It was located in the old White Building, a two-story building that stood across from the railroad depot.

The phone company was an old magneto system, and each phone had its own set of batteries. I sometimes changed out batteries, and I remember them well. They were quite large. Phone lines ran outside of Ardmore, but only a short distance; and most people were on party lines. Many people today will not remember party lines where a crank on the phone that sent a signal to everyone along the line that a call was being made. One long ring was for the operator. Long and short rings by the operator on duty signaled one of several party line members to answer the phone.

The numbers were all different. For instance the numbers 87X was one and one-half rings...a long and a short ring; 87J was two equal length rings, 87W was 3 equal length rings, 87R was for four rings, 87M was five rings and 87Y was six rings. Private lines were only in town, and they answered on one ring. These were mostly set up in local businesses or doctor's offices and residences. Needless-to-say, there wasn't much privacy on the old party lines as everyone heard every ring and often listened to other's conversations. Some operators also knew everything that was said also, but most were careful not to divulge information.

In 1948 Haney White sold the company which had about 100 customers to local resident Fountain Clay Merrell, an electrician by trade. He kept the company upstairs in the White building for some time, but then moved it into a new building owned by Mildred White on Ardmore Avenue across from Jones Drug Store. In later years, Moody King operated Moody's Barber Shop from this location. The system remained at this address until 1957 when it was moved to its present location on land purchased from local physician Dr. John Willard Maddox. Dr. Maddox's office stood next door until he retired.

In a family history printed in the 1970s, Mr. Merrell, now deceased says, "I bought the old magneto telephone plant from H. B. White for $4,500 – all on a note to pay $100 a month. Somehow, I paid it." Mr. Merrell worked to maintain the system and to give good service. As he worked at another job, he used any extra money to improve the company through the early years. Often his sons Clay and Thomas, maintenance men Howard Conner and Carl Whitsett, were out late at night trying to restore service to someone who was sick or lived alone. The service may not have been the most modern by today's standards, but it was personal and caring. Many caring operators were also available to answer a call for help. Three shifts kept the service running 24-hours per day and seven days per week year around. Operators such as Bula Troxler, Eva Neaves, Mildred and Howard Conner, Annie Puckett, Cathrine Stratton, Modena Foster Smith, and Marge Merrell later Marge McConnell, this author, and others served the community. When two switchboards were installed in the new building while waiting cut-over to the dial system in 1957, Amy Whitt, Aline Holt, Wanda Holt, Dorothy Merrell, Karen Mason, and others also served as operators. At that time two operators covered the day and early evening shifts with one operator on duty at night.

The early-to-mid 1950s were not easy times for the company. Local business owners wanted more modern service and went to the Public Service Commissions in Tennessee and Alabama with complaints, but the service was adequate for the type system and Mr. Merrell proved his case time and again. "I once went 30 days without a case of trouble," the late owner said. One group even tried to bring Southern Bell into Ardmore, but the phone giant wasn't interested in the sparsely settled rural area. There just wasn't enough potential return on their investment, and they did not try to force out a small independent company.

These people who constantly harped about their service, only served to cost the company money for attorneys to defend the company's case...money that would have been spent on improving the service.

Mr. Merrell tried to work with the locals and began searching for ways to improve the company more quickly. In 1955, he incorporated Ardmore

Telephone Company and became the first president. Other members of the board of directors were Thomas Ed Merrell, Margarette Merrell McConnell, Marie Merrell Broadway and attorney David E. Cheatam, the only non-family member stockholder. Other stockholders were Dealie F. Merrell, Clay Merrell, Loretta Merrell (Ekis), Faye Merrell (Hand). At the time the company had about 20 miles of phone lines and 230 customers.

After incorporating, the company borrowed $327,000 from the Rural Electrification Administration and began the installation of a dial plant. Mr. Merrell installed 90 miles of new wire and added customers in all four of the counties surrounding Ardmore. Before the dial system was completed, however, Mr. Merrell bought a common battery system to handle the increase in customers and installed a double switchboard in the new phone building in 1957. Some of these phones were as far away as the Tony area. Two operators worked the first two shifts and a single operator worked the night shift. As all this occurred, the company's dial plant was installed and began operating in 1958.

During the 1950s, Mr. Merrell bought the phone system in Elkmont with 82 customers, New Market with 99 customers and borrowed another $275,000 to build and install modern dial equipment there as well. The company purchased three companies in Tennessee in 1958 - Dellrose with 108 customers, Minor Hill with 185 and Boonshill with 127 customers bringing the total number of customers to 831 by the end of 1958. Mr. Merrell also had an option to purchase Madison, Alabama's phone system, but when he sold the company, the new owners opted out – a big mistake perhaps as Madison has grown significantly from that time to present day.

On March 1, 1958, with the dial system almost ready to switch into service and all lines built, Mr. Merrell sold Ardmore Telephone Company to three men from Tennessee and retired. These three men were Lee O. Brayton Jr., David Nunn and K.W. Rogers Jr. A fourth partner was Mr. Phillip Edmondson from Cornersville, TN. Mr. Edmondson became the local manager of the company for a number of years.

Between 1970 and 1976, each exchange was rebuilt and served approximately 2,600 customers, according to information printed in a book, "Telephones for Tennessee." The book printed in 1995 states that there were 8,000 customers as of that date in the four counties surrounding Ardmore in Alabama and Tennessee. By that date, both Rogers and Brayton were deceased, but Nunn retained ownership of the company.

The company has since been sold to a new owner. My nephew Tim McConnell is the only family member who works at the telephone company as of the date of this publication (2013). Tim's dad, James McConnell, also worked at the phone company as did my two brothers Clay Merrell and Thomas Merrell. It was pretty much a family operation when it was owned by the Merrell family. Tim also serves as Mayor of Ardmore, Tennessee.

Pictured Below are:
Fountain Merrell, owner and manager, and Marge Merrell, operator, about 1950 Old Magneto Switchboard at Ardmore Telephone Company, Ardmore, Tennessee

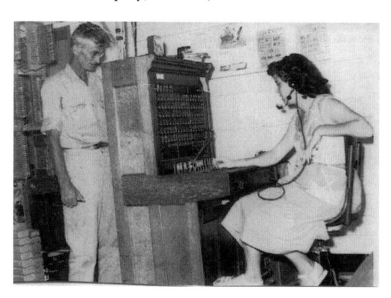

This switchboard was in use when Fountain Merrell purchased the company in 1948.

Taught To The Tune Of The Hickory Stick...

I started school in the summer of 1944. As I recall school started about mid-July and was in session for about six weeks, then broke again for fall cotton picking in Lincoln County, Tennessee where I lived. Cash Point Elementary was not air conditioned. In fact, I don't know of any place in the 1940s that was. Starting school in July meant hot rooms with little air stirring, but we were all used to the heat and humidity. We just weren't used to having to wear school clothes when it was so hot. That was the main difference, but we lived to tell about it.

The school I attended was about two miles from my home, and I had to ride an old wooden bus to school each day. I remember it was dark blue on the outside, and the three benches that ran down the length of the bus were painted the same color. No point in buying different color inside or out especially since it was probably painted in the depression years.

Those benches were not the easiest thing to sit on as the bus started up or came to a stop because you slid either forward or backward. I don't recall much about the bus except for the seats. I can't remember who the driver was during my early years, but I knew all the kids because they were either related to me or related to someone who was. As someone has said, scratch a Southerner and you'll find someone you're related to. I never had to scratch deep to find them. They were all around.

The seats on that bus were worn slick, fortunately, by all the bottoms that had slid back and forth on them for years before I started to school. I'm sure it was the same bus that my older sisters had ridden to Cash Point. Even though I wore dresses to school, I never felt a splinter.

Our school was built in a modified T shape. The first and second grade classroom formed a short base for the wider cross bar of the T which housed the 3rd-8th grades. The 3rd through 8th grades were split into two rooms, with grades 3-5 in one classroom and 6-8 in the other. There were floor to ceiling sliding, folding doors that opened when we had morning chapel, which was held every morning before school started. All the grades joined together for this morning ritual.

During chapel, one of the teachers would read a passage from the Bible. We would sing patriotic or Christian hymns and pledge allegiance to the flag of the United States. Back in the 1940s, the words "under God" had not yet been added to the pledge. However, we lived with the idea that we lived "under God" every day of our lives. As country kids, we were taught this from birth. After chapel, the doors between the middle and upper elementary classes were closed for the remainder of the day, unless one teacher sent the other a note by a student. The 1st and 2nd grades returned to their classrooms to learn their letters, numbers and as the year progressed to read about Jack and Jill. It was a simple life. We didn't have the little Blueback speller that my parents used, and thank heavens for that. I purchased a copy of that book years ago, and I couldn't believe how much more difficult it was than the books we used at the same grade level. Our parents were better educated then than some high school students are now.

There were a couple of added features to the school, but neither of them were bath rooms. There were two outhouses, one for boys and one for girls that graced the landscape. Each was a white wooden structure. The toilets did have concrete floors, and metal lids that closed on the 3 seats. During the summer the stench was awful, and you learned early on to wait until absolutely necessary to enter those buildings and then exit as quickly as possible. It did not smell like roses in those places—the stench was pretty bad despite efforts by the county schools to keep them sweeter smelling. I was always afraid of the bugs, spiders and snakes that might have slithered into the building, and I entered with trepidation each time I had to go. I think we were supplied with rolls of toilet tissue. I'm not certain since I spent as little time in those places as possible. Wintertime wasn't much better. The seats were freezing cold, and though the bugs were missing, the stench was still prevalent. Sprinkling lime on the waste may have helped, but not much.

After using the bathroom, we had to go back into the building to wash our hands. We had a sink with a water faucet in the cloakroom. There was no hot water, and in the winter the water was icy cold and equally as hot in the summer. It also had a foul taste from standing in the metal pipes. There were two faucets. One was a drinking faucet and the other for washing hands. Naturally, there were many accidents with that drinking faucet, planned and otherwise. If you weren't careful, you would spray yourself and half the cloakroom. Many a day I sat in class with a soaked blouse after getting a drink. Of course, if you were washing your hands before heading back into class, some wiseacre boy was always around to make sure you were soaked.

Another feature of the school building was the area behind the stage in the 6th-8th grade classroom. It was made so that you could access it through doors on either side of the stage, and it had another door that went down about three steps into the old cloakroom. There were times when boys would attempt to leave the classroom through the stage doors and sneak outside through the cloakroom, but the teacher in the 1st and 2nd grade classroom could always see them except in the dead of winter when her doors were closed.

I admit that I was a bit on the mischievous side when I was in the 8th grade. I had been really good until that year, and something just seemed to click in me one day that said, stop being a goody two-shoes. So I did—for one day or maybe two at most. A couple of girls and I were in the backstage area doing something, but I'm uncertain what, and we saw a wooden ladder leaning against the building underneath one of the windows. I don't know whose idea it was, but I do know that I was either the first or second to climb out the window and down that ladder, which would have been about 14 feet off the ground, if I had to make a guess. We were having a high old time, until Miss McAfee, the lady from Fayetteville who taught 4-H-Club, drove up. We thought sure she had seen us, but apparently she had her mind on something else. We hid behind shrubs until she went into the building then we shinnied up that ladder and into the backstage area faster than you can imagine. Apparently, no one ever caught us because we didn't hear anything about it then or later. I thought it was a close call, and I decided that it was not productive to do that again. Besides, my Mama and Daddy had always promised me that if I ever got a whipping at school I would have a second one when I got home. I knew they meant it. Back then, people didn't spare the rod and spoil the child. It is very different today. We were never beaten, but let's just say, we were reminded.

I do remember being in a children's play that was presented at night. I suppose that was so all the farming dads and moms could attend. I was the little girl in the play because I was small for my age. I can't recall who the mother and daddy were, but I remember insisting that both my parents attend. I doubt that I had more than 10 words to say, but it was my first acting job, and I wanted them there. They were. It was my debut to acting, and fortunately my last curtain call as well.

There were other instances at Cash Point that bring a smile to my face when I think about them. For instance, there was a school bell on a tall post outside the 8th grade classroom windows. A rope was attached to the bell so that it could be rung when recess was over to bring the kids back inside. The principal of the school was usually in charge of this activity.

However, when he was absent, a substitute teacher, usually Mrs. Iona Roper, would come in and that was when the fun began. This lady always brought an alarm clock with her to keep track of when to start and stop classes, let us out for recess, and call us back in. Always, and I don't think it ever failed; someone in the upper classes would be assigned the duty of changing the clock to benefit the students. Since she had three classes to teach, someone from another class would advance the hands on the old alarm clock so that she would let us out early for recess. Then another partner in crime would sneak in while she was talking with one of the other teachers and move the hands back so as to extend recess. This happened a few times until she got smart and kept the clock right beside her. That didn't stop kids from grabbing the bell rope and tossing it outside so that it couldn't be reached. The only way they could get us all back inside was to go out and round up each group of kids on the playground. Since the boys went to the backside of the playground to a grove of trees, it was a long hike to get them in. I'm sure this poor woman wondered why she ever signed up to be a sub at Cash Point. Mrs. Roper was a sweet little lady, but we didn't cut her any slack for being nice. But then kids don't always behave when they know they can get away with it.

One of my teachers played the accordion, and when he learned I was taking accordion lessons, he often invited himself to my parent's house. He and my dad, who also played, had a grand old time playing together, but I was often embarrassed in case someone saw him coming or going from our home. In hindsight it was silly to worry about it. I was afraid they would think I was a teacher's pet because I did make good grades, but it had nothing to do with him visiting my parents.

We didn't have any play equipment in grade school except for a couple of seesaws and 3 swings that hung from a huge tree limb. We did have balls and bats and a makeshift ball field, but mostly we played games such as dodge ball, red rover or jump rope. I can remember swinging as high as I could go and then jumping out as the swing arced to the highest point. I probably did more damage to my bone structure than I could imagine, but it was something we all did. I've seen my grandkids do the same thing, so I guess it was just a kid thing.

I was good at jump rope, swinging, dodge ball and red rover, but I was terrible at softball. I was very small for my age, and even though I could run as fast as a roadrunner, I could not catch, hit, or throw a ball far enough to be effective. Part of my problem was that I was nearsighted, and I feared getting hit in the face by a ball. I was always one of the last to be chosen by a team because I could not play well. The kids in the older grades always made me run for them. They would hit the ball, but I'd run the bases for them. I was always a fast runner, and I have scars on my aging knees today from a bet made with one of my classmates who was also small and a fast runner.

This particular classmate was visiting our home with her parents, and one of us challenged the other to a foot race. We took off flying through our big front yard, and I did win by a hair; but I paid a price. I did not slow down as I approached the barbed wire fence at one end of the yard that separated the cow pasture from the yard. She apparently did, but I was determined to win and didn't break my speed. I plowed into that barbed wire fence and won the contest. You might say that I also won the biggest idiot award as well since I destroyed my knees in the process. Pride cometh before a fall...or maybe after a barbed wire fence.

I remember one incident at school that embarrassed me. For some reason, we had bottles of indelible ink and fountain pens we were allowed to use in one of the upper classes. There were no ballpoint pens in those days, so we had to fill the pens with ink. My friend, Clara Mae Cross, and I were filling our pens, and somehow I managed to knock the ink off on her dress. She and I walked to her home, which was about a mile or more from school so that she could change dresses. Mrs. Cross was so nice about this even though it was a new dress. I really did feel so bad about that incident, and it has stayed with me throughout the years. I suspect the teacher had me go home with Clara Mae because I was the guilty party. I never thought of that back then. I was just embarrassed about my error.

Our little school house was a great place to bond with friends, and for the most part it was a good place to grow up. However, as much as the teachers tried, our school rooms were not blessed with many library books, and I was always searching for reading material. I never felt that I had the best education in elementary school because of the lack of reading material. I look at the advantages my own children had and my grandchildren have today, and I realize the only thing we actually had was good, dedicated teachers. Since we were in the very southwest end of our county, no one ever paid much attention to our needs. That we grew and learned at all is a testament to those teachers and our parents who sacrificed to keep us in school so that we could become educated.

I suppose it worked. Most of us turned out to be productive citizens. We could read, write, comprehend, and solve arithmetic problems; so we must have learned something. It was just a bit more difficult than it should have been for all concerned. When I hear parents talking today about the need for new books, better facilities, etc., I think how blessed kids are to have so many advantages. But I also realize that much of the learning process doesn't hinge on "things," but on the teachers and students. If you want to learn, you will learn. You may not have all the fancy equipment, but you can and will learn if you put forth the effort. That is something today's parents should consider when they are screaming at their school boards.

Today students are taught with the use of not only old fashioned teaching methods but the newer electronic gadgets. There is absolutely nothing wrong with this, and I think students do benefit from the use of technology in the schools. However, it bothers me when I see students who cannot read when they've finished high school, or worse still can't work a fairly simple math problem. I won't even mention the lack of not knowledge of English and how to speak and use it.

When the boards of education are forced to dumb down classes in order to mainstream every child, all children suffer. There should be separate classes for those who fall behind for any reason. It is unfair to these children as well as all others if they are not helped as needed. Also, when our federal government mandates that every child must pass certain exams to be promoted, they lose even more. Let's turn our public schools back to the local boards of education and remove some of the federal mandates from the agenda. I fully believe, after years of covering education board meetings and listening to educators, that you would finally see kids actually educated rather than processed through 12 or 13 grades. Please, don't blame the teachers in every case. Most of them are working hard to educate your child. Support the teachers and your local boards. Work together and make sure your child is adequately supported by your own efforts. Get off your couch and work with your children. Don't expect the schools to teach them everything they need to know in life.

During my school years, corporal punishment was permitted in schools, and kids learned to behave or they ended up in the principal's office for some "board time." There were no time outs for miscreants. No psychology was used. If you did the crime, you were punished. I don't advocate teachers paddle students today because there is too much room for abuse, but I do think that they should have some way to discipline kids who disrupt classrooms and cause teachers to lose precious time with all the students.

We moved to Western Kentucky for the better part of two years when I was in the 8th grade, and I met a wonderful teacher from Giles County, TN at that school. Mrs. Springer taught English at Heath High School. Many years later, Heath High School was the scene of a student who went on a killing rampage. At the time I was there, it was a really good school located just outside of Paducah, KY. I loved going to school at Heath where I met some wonderful friends, one of whom I've located in the past few years. I never forgot Carole Huff and Carolyn Osgood. Carole was from Spiro, OK and Carolyn was from El Paso, TX. They were super nice girls, and I'm so proud to have become friends with them even for a brief time. People in our lives leave an imprint, and I'm happy to say both Carole and Carolyn left a wonderful imprint on my life. Carole now lives back in Oklahoma where she has a husband and family. I located her because her brother was a superintendent of schools near the Oklahoma City area. When I Googled her brother's name, whom I remembered, I found his bio and his sister Carole was listed with her married name. I was thrilled and have been in touch with her since. As they say new friends are silver, but old friends are gold. Indeed they are. I lost track of Carolyn, but I have never forgotten them along with all my childhood friends.

When we moved back to our home in Lincoln County outside Ardmore, I was happy to be reunited with my friends from elementary school, and really enjoyed the new friends I made at Blanche High School where I graduated. I loved Blanche, and I have always enjoyed attending my class reunions. We were a relatively small class, but we all got along well. They are family to me. I am thankful for having them in my life. I have so many beautiful memories of my school days. Basketball was our school's strength as far as sports went, and I still love basketball today. Only today I root for the University of Kansas Jayhawks because that is where my son went to college and now my two granddaughters are students there. I've seen many changes in life, but I really do appreciate the life I've lived, both in and out of the South

One memory of school days that I must share is my love of new books. When I was in elementary school, we had to buy our own school books. The state didn't start furnishing books until we were in high school; so that meant each summer we had to make a trip to a store on the courthouse square in Fayetteville, TN to buy books for the coming year.

This trip excited me far more than the yearly visit to the county fair because I couldn't wait to get books to study and read, and I always did even though I was admonished to save them for school. I would sit down with my textbooks and read them from one end to the other. My math books never had a mark in them, except for my name, but I would work every problem I could before school started. By the time school began, I already knew most of the material, but I still listened in class. I suspect this self-study enabled me to sail through my classes without difficulty every year. I never thought of it as getting a jump on homework. I simply loved to read and study. That urge stayed with me until I hit about 70, and since then I've been less inclined to study hard. I still learn, but I don't pursue learning as I once did. The years have a way of catching up with you.

Reading and writing were the two things I really wanted to learn, and once I did, I was off and running. Writing my own themes in school was duck soup, and writing them for other classmates was just as easy. I truly never realized how blessed I was to be able to read and write well until many, many years later. It was only when I began volunteering in my son's elementary school that I realized the value of these two gifts. There are some who cannot read well or write well, and I will always have a soft spot for these children who try so hard and can only accomplish so little.

I learned more about WWII by reading than perhaps was good for me at the time. My brother Clay went into the Air Force after high school, and being an avid reader of history, he purchased a full set of books that were like encyclopedias with stories about the war years of the 1940s. They had many photos as well. These books must have been printed in the late 40s because I was only about 13 when I started reading them, and I did read them all the way through...all 10-12 volumes of them. It was in those books that I learned of man's inhumanity to man because there were many graphic photos of people piled into giant holes in the ground after having been gassed in Hitler's effort to rid the world of the Jewish race. Today when someone tells me they don't believe the holocaust destroyed millions, I want to tell them they are crazy. I saw photos that were made during that time period, and I know that Hitler was a tyrant who destroyed many and took all that belonged to them. That is why I find it so important today that we know what our government is doing, what direction it wants to take us and whether there is someone in the seat of power who would, if permitted, become a dictator. As is often said, if you don't know history, you are doomed to repeat it. So I encourage everyone to read your history. Insist the schools teach your children the history of this country and world. Many kids do not like history, but it can be made interesting if the teacher presents the material in a manner that is digestible for their students. I had a history teacher in high school who while a decent teacher never did a great job of making the subject matter palatable to most of her students. For her it was more about memorizing dates and places when the real reason for events was left mostly for the students to ferret out on their own. Sadly, she probably turned off more students to history than any other thing would have.

The Old School Song

School days, school days

Dear old Golden Rule days

'Reading and 'riting and 'rithmetic

Taught to the tune of the hick'ry stick

You were my queen in calico

I was your bashful, barefoot beau

And you wrote on my slate, "I Love You So"

When we were a couple o' kids

Written by Will Cobb and Jess Edwards in 1907 (public domain)

By the time my generation was in school, there were no more slates used, only blackboards. However, the hickory stick in the form of a paddle was still in use. I'll bet some of those kids well remember those paddles, too--especially the boys.

Blacklisted, Spanked and Other Elementary Antics

Early in my school years, I found myself blacklisted. No, I was neither a disruptive child nor an ornery one. In fact, I was the type of child who would bend over backwards to follow all the rules. But I was the victim of a teacher who apparently trusted no one, especially the small children in her classroom. I won't name the teacher because she is no longer living to defend herself, but she made a mark on me that I've carried through life. Not a physical mark, but an emotional mark, which is sometimes far worse than being hit with a hickory stick…I've felt the sting of both, and I far prefer the hickory stick.

This teacher, whom I'll call Ms. Doe, was known for her strict discipline, perhaps as much so as for her ability to teach. At any rate, I was a good student. I sat quietly in class, did my lessons and made A's on my report card. I was never marked down for deportment. I wasn't an angel, I'm sure of that, but I was never in trouble. However, that apparently didn't count in this class.

Since Daddy worked out of town during the week, and my brothers and I had to help plant the garden, our mother told us to come home at lunchtime to help plant potatoes one spring day. My brothers who were about four and six years older than me would prepare the soil, and I was to help drop the potatoes so they could be covered. I told my teacher when I got to school that morning that I needed to go home to help plant the potatoes. My brothers and I walked the two miles home from school, but when we got home we learned that the soil was too wet. There was no reason to head back to school since it would have taken another 40 minutes or more to get there. We didn't have a car at home. Mama told us to come home the next day because the soil should be ready then.

Remember we were country kids and used to working the land, and my teacher was raised on a farm, so she should have realized that the soil had to be right for planting. Anyway, the next morning, I told her I needed to

65

go home at lunchtime again to plant potatoes and explained why. Apparently, she was having a really bad day, and she decided on the spot that I was lying. She called me a liar and said she had no use for someone who did lie. She said that I could not go home with my brothers. Furthermore, she said she was putting me on a "blacklist." She had put other students on the blacklist, and I knew what that meant. It was pretty severe punishment for a young child. I had to sit at my small desk, except to go to the bath room a couple of times a day, for a week. I was not allowed to talk to anyone except to answer the teacher if she asked me a question. I could not go outside at lunchtime or for morning and afternoon recess. I was not allowed to draw or color pictures. In other words, I was a POW in the classroom, and I felt that blow harder than if she had beaten me. The child in me today still morns for the understanding I didn't get from her.

I was a very sensitive child, and I had been taught by my parents not to lie and to obey the rules. I had not committed a sin, but I felt that I was as black as her blacklist, which by the way had my name written in huge letters on her blackboard along with BLACKLISTED...thus, the black list. I was so humiliated and ashamed. To this day when someone accuses me of something that I did not do, I lose it. I think back to those days on the blacklist when I was treated as if I were the biggest sinner in the world. Did I hate my teacher? No, I did not hate her, but I lost respect for her that day, and I couldn't wait for my time to pass so that I could get out of her classes. We only had three teachers in our tiny school. One taught first and second grades, another third through fifth and another sixth through eighth grades. So I was in her class for more than one year, and I went to school each day during those years filled with dread. That is not a good learning environment for any child.

Being placed on this blacklist for several days left an emotional imprint on me, which is difficult to describe. I don't even remember if I told my Mother about the incident. She would have had no way of knowing if I didn't because teachers didn't communicate with parents in those days. My brothers wouldn't have known anything other than I didn't get to help plant the potatoes that day, and they wouldn't have cared one way or the other. So, I bore my burden alone, but I had nightmares in early elementary school about being put on a blacklist, and it has followed me to some degree all my life.

It wasn't until I began to mature that I started to develop a slightly thicker skin. It became necessity when I worked on a newspaper because there were always politicians who would call my boss and tell them that things I wrote were not factual, and nothing made me angrier. I have never knowingly lied about any news that I reported, and I would stand up for myself when attacked. To this day, if someone attacks me, I don't cower and allow myself to be pushed around as I did in elementary school. Perhaps I learned a good lesson from those days, but to a young kid in early elementary school, it was an emotional lesson I should not have had to learn.

Emotional abuse in children is often difficult to detect. Hidden scars from child abuse often manifest themselves in numerous behavioral ways such as insecurity, poor self-esteem, destructive behavior, anger and acts of cruelty toward other children or animals, withdrawal, poor development of social skills, drug abuse, alcohol, suicide, difficulty in forming and sustaining relationships and unstable job histories.

So to all parents I say, guard and protect your children against abuse by anyone, whether a teacher, friend, preacher or anyone who has authority over them. If your child tells you something is wrong, listen closely and if they need your intervention, don't hesitate. I'm just thankful the abuse ended for me without a great deal of scarring, but I still felt the effects for many years. It made me distrustful of others and caused me to believe I had to be perfect to gain someone's love. Those scars are still there, but with help I've overcome most. Yet, it will always be with me to some degree.

The only spanking I ever receive in school, and spankings were allowed in school throughout my 12 years, was given to me by Mrs. Annie Lee Hill. Miss Annie Lee, as we called her, was related to me through my Reed side of the family, and I did like her. She was always good to me and very helpful throughout my three years in her classroom. She taught 3rd – 5th grades.

She wasn't absent much doing my three years in her class room, but one day she had to have a sub come in to take over the classes. This woman was a local teacher, and we all knew her to some degree. Unfortunately, she wasn't able to subdue a room full of grade school kids, as is often the case for a sub.

She tried, but there were some unruly kids in that room. I was not one of them. I might have talked a bit more than normal, but I don't remember even doing that. I know that I was not into trouble that day. I always made sure I didn't offend the teacher or substitute teacher who came in. Anyway, it was a chaotic day with the boys pulling stunts on each other and some of the girls chiming in. I'm sure the teacher was exhausted when she left for the day, and she no doubt promised herself she'd never come back. But that wasn't the end of it.

The next day Miss Annie Lee came in and said she had heard of the actions of the class, and she told us that everyone involved was going to be spanked. She said if we had been in trouble to line up, and like a silly goose, I got into line with all the other kids even though I really hadn't done anything. Only one girl, Sarah Francis Mitchell, did not get in line. I should have opted out as she did, but I was not going to run the chance of being blacklisted by yet another teacher, so I took my spanking as did all the others.

However, when I got to the teacher, she just tapped me lightly on my behind with her paddle and told me to behave myself. She knew I didn't act up in class, and she knew I could be trusted. I'm sure she also knew that I was simply trying to stay out of trouble when I joined that discipline line.

I never received another spanking at school, nor did I ever get disciplined. However, there were times when I should have been…well, maybe.

Of course, one of our favorite things to do in the upper grades was to collect all the blackboard erasers and take them out to the well house and beat the chalk dust out of them at the close of the day. That was always fun because we could laugh and talk without getting in trouble out on the playground.

When I was in the 9th grade at Heath High School in Kentucky where we were living in 1953, two of my best friends did get into trouble, minor but trouble, nevertheless. As I recall, and my memory may be a bit rusty on this, but it seems we had finished PE and were in the girl's bathroom before going to English class, when the incident occurred.

One of the girls, and I don't know which one, found a tube of toothpaste and thought how funny it would be to squirt the toothpaste behind the radiator in the bathroom. I was neither the instigator nor the person who did the squirting, but I do remember standing over by one of the sinks and laughing…which made me an accessory I suppose. Anyway, I realized they might get in trouble, so I quickly left the room and went upstairs to my class arriving maybe a couple minutes late. Fortunately, it was Mrs. Springer's class, and she always seemed to favor me and didn't say anything when I sat down.

Not long after I left the bathroom and left them holding the tube, someone in authority walked in and caught them. The next day they were sent downstairs to clean the girl's bathroom. I hated they got caught, but I would have hated it a whole lot worse had I been in the midst of it when the teacher came in. Had I been involved in the escapade, I would have been disciplined both at school and at home. You might call that double jeopardy, but that is the way my parents felt about kids acting out in school.

Anyway, although I thought their antics were funny, I was very happy that I didn't stick around to see what kind of mess was made. My gut instinct told me to get out of there, and I did. I realize that these antics seem very minor compared to the things kids often try or actually do in school today, but we were not malicious or vindictive. We were just kids, who while knowing better, allowed temptation to take over. I'm sure that if I had been caught I would have been singing a totally different tune today.

I can't recall doing anything like that after the one scare in Kentucky. By and large, I was always one to obey the rules or the laws. I'm still pretty much that way. If there is a sign that says "stay off grass," I will not walk on the grass. I'll go out of my way to avoid it. It's just the way I am made. I never had any desire to get into real trouble. I've never taken drugs of any sort, unless prescribed by a doctor; and I've never smoked pot. As far as I'm concerned, rules are not suggestions. Perhaps that is why I'm very conservative today. So be it.

On the following page are two photos made at Cash Point Elementary School. The top photo is the upper classes in 1952. The bottom photo is of the lower classes that same year.

Above two photos are courtesy of Peggy Hargrave Holt.

The Dead Will Rise Again

As a child, I remember the older folks "laying out and sitting up with the dead." Funeral homes were not common before the 1930s in our area. There was one funeral home in the area, but they were only used for transporting the body to the church and cemetery for the burial. Sometimes, the hearse did double duty as an ambulance, but for the most part, the last ride most people made was to the cemetery. In the early '30s, it might have been their one and only ride in a horseless carriage.

When a family member died, the woman of the house usually cleaned and dressed the body for burial, which included washing and combing the hair. Beauticians weren't called in to make the body look beautiful. When you died, you went home to God in clothing that was from your own wardrobe. Sometimes when there wasn't anything left that was decent for burial purposes, clothing would be purchased, but it wasn't often that happened. Another tradition was placing pennies on the eyelids of the dead to keep the eyes closed. Guess no one wanted the eyelid to pop open in the middle of the night and send the "sitters" into hysterics or worse.

After electricity was run throughout the Tennessee Valley, people sitting up with the dead could have lights in the room where they were sitting with the dead. Before that, I'm sure it was kerosene lamps or oil lamps as we often referred to them. Having used those kind of lamps during power outages, I can attest to the fact that the light provided is better than nothing, but the smell of burning kerosene is not something to enjoy

When someone died, neighbors would come to the home of the deceased and sit through the night "guarding" the body. This was not only to show respect for the person but also a protection against possible invasion of rodents or other varmints since many were not embalmed before burial. Today, most people are embalmed and kept in a very cool room at the funeral parlor until the funeral is held. Perhaps that is more humane, but it is a bit sad in some respects.

Graves were often dug by family members or close friends of the deceased. A death in the neighborhood was a death in the "family." Everyone pitched in and helped. Later when funeral homes took over the laying out and burying of the dead, folks tended to not show up at the home of the deceased but waited to pay their respects at the funeral home. Today, a funeral may bring hordes of people who will stand in a reception line for an hour or more to walk past the bier and shake a family member's hand, but you won't find them providing much other support to the family. If you are a member of the church or live in a small community, people will bring food for the family. I don't know how this custom began, but it is a very helpful one for the family who is not thinking about putting food on the table at that time.

Long before my maternal grandmother died in 1961, she hand made her own dress and underwear for her funeral. She didn't want to be a burden to anyone when she departed this world. Today, many people buy special clothing, but when you really get down to it, it is kind of useless to get dressed up for an event you don't know you are attending. As my Daddy always said, give me my flowers while I live. When I pass on, it won't matter much what you do because I'm not going to be there to see it. But such is our Southern way…dressing up the dead for their last ride. It gives new meaning to the old saying: "All dressed up and nowhere to go." Except does it? Our faith tells us we're making the most important journey of our life. Of course, our real reason for dressing our loved ones is so that no one will go away from the funeral saying, "Bless her heart, did you see what they buried her in?"

However, I've known of people who were buried in the uniforms they worked in every day, but most people put their loved ones in their Sunday best to go to meet the Lord. For me, I just want to be dressed in my faith in the Lord. He'll take care of the rest. Of course, I do hope that someone actually does clothe me. I wouldn't want anyone to faint at the sight of an old, spent carcass lying in a casket.

Today large funeral homes have taken over the death business. They not only hold the body there for two or three days, but they offer a chapel, music and coffee for the mourners for a price. No one sits overnight with the body, but a visitation or viewing period, the nomenclature depends on where you live, is held so that family and friends can express their condolences.

I've actually stood in line for more than an hour to simply walk through quickly and shake the family member's hands. It is amazing how many people will show up for a funeral in the South. If you pass a funeral home, and a long, snaking line has formed outside in the parking lot, you can be assured that the deceased is either well known, rich or has a big family. The longer the receiving line the more prominent the individual who died, or so it would seem. However, prominence doesn't necessarily mean money. It is more likely the person had a large family, and in the South we have a lot of kissing kin. We are often a tight knit bunch in the South, and no one dies without being soundly honored and respected no matter what their station in life. People in the South will always find something good to say about the person and will support the family.

Funerals bring friends and family together as nothing else can in the South unless it is a covered dish dinner at church or a football game. When we get together, we laugh, tell stories about the deceased (always nice stories) and help to cheer one another as best we can. Hearing laughter at a visitation isn't disrespectful as it might seem. It is simply our way of helping one another get through a difficult time.

If you've ever noticed, preachers often use a funeral to get the attention of the unsaved or the back-slider in the audience. I suppose you could say that they never let a good funeral go to waste, so they preach to both the choir and to those who need to be in church but often aren't. Sometimes, it is their only chance to tell the lost about the Lord, and it may be the first time some have heard a sermon since their mothers took them to church. You can't fault a preacher for that. He's doing his job.

Funeral music in the south is typically favorite hymns of the deceased. The family often arranges for music and singing. Depending on your religious affiliation, you get sent home to glory acapella or with musical instruments. Some of the favorites at funerals are "In the Garden," "Amazing Grace," "Till We Meet Again," and my favorite, "How Great

Thou Art." There have been some rather unusual things happen at a funeral by accident and by design.

I remember sitting in the chapel of a local funeral home and hearing Johnny Cash singing something that sounded like "I Walk The Line." Yes, there was country music coming through the speakers even after the body was rolled into the front of the chapel. Fortunately, someone discovered the music, and a more somber tune was soon wafting through the chapel. Another funeral was unusual by design for a very young man who died suddenly. It seems that the songs for that funeral were his favorite rock songs. I think that would have been a bit disturbing, but each to his own. When I'm flying away to meet my maker, I don't want to hear Elvis Pressley singing, "Jailhouse rock." Floyd Cramer's Last Date might be appropriate though.

Today you don't often hear a lot of sobbing at funerals. We as a society abhor making a display of ourselves, so we do our crying behind closed doors. We don't want to make a scene that would reflect badly on the deceased. I remember at one visitation when a young woman walked in who hadn't spoken to her relative in years and began wailing like a banshee. Though they lived in the same city, they never visited. Since that is not the norm, it rather surprised those in attendance. I thought it was a fire alarm at first, but soon realized that the noise was coming from near the casket. It was a bit disconcerting, but we each express sorrow in various ways. If she felt like wailing, then more power to her. Grieving is natural, and if you feel like crying then cry. It is no one's business.

When the Lord calls me home, I hope that I am prepared to meet him. When I think of the new heaven and new earth that awaits me, the saints who will welcome me home, I'm overcome with joy. If you can imagine a world without sin, walking and talking with the Lord, then you can imagine heaven. Though I love this life on earth, I eagerly await the day when I will be in God's presence and singing with the heavenly choir. Of course, there is an awful lot of work the Lord has to do to be to get me ready for the choir. No doubt about it. I just hope that he sees fit to forgive me for my all my joking and nonsense through the years.

Dancing, Drinking and other sins of the Flesh

Growing up in the Bible belt South, I was taught that drinking was a sin, and dancing was the devil's way of getting boys and girls in trouble. I was probably in the minority, but I neither drank nor danced as a teen, except for square dancing with girls during PE at school, which was permitted, and doing the Charleston with my brother-in-law James in the living room of my parent's home.

Southern boys have always been able to get their hands on liquor, even if they had to buy it from a bootlegger or from some guy's still back in the woods. It was probably one of their ways of making a homely girl look beautiful, or to gain courage to do things they should not do. But I am not male so that is only conjecture on my part.

Southern girls, on the other hand, were taught that drinking and dancing would lead to pregnancy, so we avoided both as if they were the plague. At least, the girls I knew well did. That didn't stop the boys from drinking and trying their best to entice girls to drink. I can say with all honesty I didn't drink, though we had a neighbor lady who would give us kids a spoonful of homemade wine on rare occasions. I detested the smell of alcohol on someone's breath, and I disliked what it caused them to do even more. I can't think of anything more disgusting than the silly look on a drunk's face just before he tosses the contents of his stomach all over himself.

Once in Huntsville, I saw some boys and girls at a hamburger joint in downtown Huntsville giving beer to a poor, starving kitten. That little kitten was staggering around all over the place, and I wanted to get out of the car and bop them over the head. It was disgusting, but they were so drunk they thought it was funny. I didn't. I still wish I had done as I wanted to do, but I was too timid.

While growing up in Ardmore, I often heard stories about the wild men and women who indulged themselves in the sport of drinking and dancing. The place they frequented had an appropriate name, Bloody Bucket, since it was infamous for the fights that often brought police to the scene.

Southern Ways and Southern Days

My parents never went to taverns, and we were threatened within an inch of our lives if we ever did. However, they didn't have to worry. I didn't even know anyone who went to taverns—until I worked as a telephone operator during high school, then I heard about girls in Ardmore going. I've often wondered why so many men and women go to these places to meet an eligible man or woman? You think they would know that a person who hangs out at those places night after night isn't always good marriage material. That one issue never seems to cross their minds. In my youth, nice girls didn't go to taverns...period. At least, that was the way it was in my family. I can't speak for the younger generations, but if they went, it certainly wasn't considered something to brag about.

Once when my husband, Bob, and I moved to Seattle, Bob wanted to drop by a place called The 19th Hole, to see a fellow who had worked for him at Boeing in Huntsville. The guy decided there was more money to be made in a bar than helping build defense weapons, so when he was laid off in 1970, that is what he did. Ray was a nice man, and he and his wife were often guests at our house for dinner. However, since owning the tavern, he didn't get out socially anymore, and Bob had missed seeing him.

To make a long story short, I argued with Bob about going into such a place, but he said it was nice and quiet and no one would say anything to me. Once inside, I could see it was nothing like the horror stories I'd heard about Bloody Bucket, but I still felt very out of place and was anxious to leave. I was as nervous as a cat on a hot tin roof.

Before going into the place, a woman pulled up as we were walking in, and asked me to tell her husband she was waiting outside. She described him, and I easily spotted him at the bar since there were only three other men there. I wanted to help the woman since she had her hair in big white rollers and looked fairly casual in her dress so I walked over to him and told him his wife said she was waiting in the car. The man glared at me and said, I don't give a #!@*^$! what she's doing, I ain't leaving." With that I quickly walked away with my face flashing neon red. How embarrassing! I learned a lesson. One--don't go to a tavern, but if you get dragged there by a well-meaning husband, don't speak to anyone. The other thing I learned is that many wives may sit outside and wait for their husbands to end their "happy hour", but I won't deliver a message again. Fortunately for me, Bob didn't stay more than five minutes talking to his friend, and we were out of there.

Another time when I was working for the newspaper in Ardmore, I was asked to go to the old 31 Blue Spot (the former Bloody Bucket) and take a picture of the Toys for Tots Marine charity kick-off. I was supposed to go at 8 a.m., but I didn't want to darken the door. I argued with my boss about it, and told him I didn't want to go to that tavern that had been the subject of many stories in my youth. He told me no one would bother me, so I did. Fortunately, the tavern was not open to the public, and only the owner and the Marine were there. I took the pictures and left quickly. It was my one and only time to have been in that tavern. I felt guilty as sin just going in to take the photo, and I suspect my parents would have laughed at me for being so foolish. It wasn't the building that was forbidden…it was the actions of those who went that made it a place you didn't want to be, but then it's hard to get over teachings that have played themselves over and over in your head from childhood.

I realize it is the way people act when they are indulging themselves in alcohol that makes something sinful. Alcohol in a bottle isn't a sin, but some people should never open the bottle. The same goes for dancing. Dancing in itself isn't necessarily bad. It's some of the things that go on while dancing that creates the problem…such as suggestive movements and the desire those dances sometimes inspire. Either way, I think I was well served by having parents who discussed these things and prevented me from going there. In that way, and in many others, I was blessed with parents who had common sense, and alcohol has never been something I have felt drawn to.

Today in the Kansas City area, I sometimes go to a Bar and Grill for dinner with my family. These places are basically for families even though they sell alcohol. They are quiet and not at all like the wild taverns of my youth. The food in these places is some of the better in the area, and I've learned that sensible people go there to eat, not to get sloppy drunk. Everything in moderation appears to be the best idea when it comes to eating, drinking and any other activity in life.

I'm not someone who says you should never take a drink, but I do think that it is always wise to drink responsibly, and if you do drink, please don't drive.

That Old Time Religion...

If you grew up in the South of the 1940s and '50s, you will remember some of the same things I do about that old time religion. In those days, we grew up with a healthy respect for the Lord, our parents and teachers. Today, I'm not certain that holds true in every case. Children were taken to church whether they wanted to go or not, and if the case was not, they had better not have said it out loud to their parents. You went to church because you had been taught that your parents knew best and you were to obey them. Now how much you absorbed, depended on whether your parents were keeping a close eye on you during the service.

In my home church, I remember that the elderly men always sat in the Amen Corner. I suppose it was called this because they were always saying "Amen" when the preacher stated something they agreed with. I've often wondered if when they didn't say Amen, that it meant they didn't agree? I don't think I thought much about seeing my uncles and cousins seated in the Amen Corner while their wives sat elsewhere and the kids sat with their friends. But as I look back on it, it does seem like a strange tradition.

Our choir, unlike some churches today, was at the front of the church, and the choir would sit there all during the sermon. To be honest, the older women often sat there with clenched mouths glaring at the kids in church who were misbehaving and even some who weren't. There was one thing about it, each lady had their special seat in the choir and heaven forbid if someone took that seat even for one service.

A few times, we teens were allowed to sit in the choir, and these same women would sit in the audience and stare at us as if we had stolen their favorite cookie. Bless their hearts, I guess they meant to present a Christian example for us, but it seemed more likely they were urging us to never take their seats again. I bet if truth be known, there are still members of the choir who think a certain seat belongs to them and only them. I'll bet they would get very perturbed if they were asked to step down and allow the younger generation to take over the choir for a few weeks. Some things probably don't change, and I suspect this is one of them. In the church I attend, choir members have to try out for the choir, and the choir director is a highly educated college professor. Also, there is no choir loft. When they sing in our small church, they move from their seats in the congregation to stand near the piano then return to their seats when they finish. Sometimes it is hard to get choir members since most don't want to have to try out for a place. Me included.

I remember when Bro. Raymond Kennedy was the preacher at our church. He had been there as long as I could remember and had baptized me. When he announced he was leaving to go to Flint River Baptist Church, I was so sad. I did not understand the "call" to go somewhere else, and I really missed him after he left. He was an old fashioned Baptist preacher who wasn't afraid to call a spade a spade, slam his Bible down on the pulpit or raise his voice to get your attention. He got mine, and I'm thankful he did. He also didn't hesitate to ask the young people in the back to be quite when he was preaching either. Today so many preachers seldom raise their voice, and I find it hard to focus on monotone sermons. As has often been said, however, your mind absorbs only what your seat allows. In other words, long winded preachers may think they are getting their points across when they preach overtime, but if the seat says it is time to pack up and go home, nothing he says will be absorbed. You can almost count on that. Personally, I always figured that if a preacher talked for more than 20 minutes, he would lose the audience in the next five, and in my church that is usually the case. As the sermon nears an end, you can certainly hear a whole lot of shuffling going on.

We went to Vacation Bible School during the summer when school was in session. In the 1940s, that was a common practice where I grew up. We would march over to the church from school, form two lines and two children would be chosen to carry the American and the Christian flags into the auditorium. We often sang Onward Christian Soldier as we marched in. Inside, we pledged allegiance to both the American and Christian flags. I always enjoyed VBS, and I think children still do today. However, today it would be illegal for children to go from the school to the church for VBS during the school day. Sadly, a lot of children never hear the Bible taught or preached because their parents don't go to church and take them. Our society would be so much more civil and moral if kids were taken to church by their parents.

It used to be if you grew up in the South, you were taught to live a Christian life. I can remember as a child I knew within a 10-mile radius only one woman who was divorced. That was a word that just wasn't spoken, and most people did stay married and tried to build a good life together. I'm sure there were some not so happy marriages, but you seldom heard of anyone in the neighborhood planning to leave their husband/wife, and with few exceptions, there were few illegitimate children as well. Of course, divorce, having children outside of marriage and that sort of thing has existed for about as long as there have been human beings, but it was the exception, not the rule in our area during the 40s and 50s. For the most part, people didn't live together without legal bonds and the few who broke the rules had a bad reputation. The idea of homosexuality was never discussed when I was growing up. I never actually knew of anyone who was perceived as being homosexual. A couple of people were considered "funny" when they never married, but I'm not sure anyone thought they were of that persuasion. I didn't.

Yes, times have changed, and the South has fallen into moral decay the same as people throughout the world. Today women think nothing about bearing a man's child without being married. Young men and women think it is perfectly normal to live together without commitment. Same sex coupling is accepted. The world has accepted this as the norm, but where I came from we were taught...first comes love, then comes marriage, then comes Sally with a baby carriage...not the other way around. Nor did children have two fathers or two mothers. I wish our younger generations

83

would go back and study the Bible and see how civilizations have floundered and been destroyed due to immorality and worshipping of false gods. Yes, I did say false gods. Anytime you put something before God in your life, you are idol worshipping. Read the Old Testament, and you'll find that idolatry includes many things, not just some Buddha statue. I can hear many of you saying that I'm old and don't see the world as you do. All I can say is I'm thankful I don't see it that way. I am old fashioned and I plan to stay that way as long as God allows me to live. I do know that with age comes wisdom, and when I was younger I had as little as allowed. Now I'm older and see the fallacy of my youth.

Recently, I saw a Facebook quote that really upset me though I know that many in our society would laugh and think it funny. It was a sarcastic remark about Jesus and his "magic." God help us if this country ever reaches the Sodom and Gomorrah state, and I think we are getting close. I hope that people in this country will consider how they are throwing away the life that God gave them in order to have their drugs, immorality and their "fun."

If you are reading this book and gotten this far, you know I've never claimed to be an angel. I was well-behaved when I was growing up, but a sassy brat at times when I thought no one was listening. However, I do think that morals, good manners, and living a life pleasing to God is important. If you have children, it is your responsibility to guide and direct those children to adulthood. Remember that children are like sponges, so if you want good children, then be good parents.

Memories of the 'Singing Wheels'

As I remember, the skating rink at Ardmore was built in the early 1950s by Foster and Zelma (Miss Polly) Magnusson. At the time, it was named Singing Wheels Skating Rink, and as more and more kids learned to keep their balance on those hardwood floors, the wheels did sing.

The rink was open air, meaning that the panels covering the rink were open when skating was in session to allow for ventilation during the summer months. In the winter, on-lookers, and there were many, had to move indoors to watch the kids and young adults flying by "on a wing and a prayer."

It was always interesting to see new skaters on the floor. One spill could send half a dozen into a pile up—think NASCAR pile-ups. No one ever seemed much worse for the wear though. Young bodies healed quickly from minor scrapes and pain. Of course, newbie's often fared far worse than anyone else on the rink as more experienced skaters gave them a wide birth and in some cases were able to cross over a protruding leg or arm in order to avoid hurting them. New skaters either hugged the rail or got tangled in someone else's skates, but after a few sessions they were going round and round and more sure-footed. Sometimes more experienced skaters also got their feet tangled, but not as often as new skater's. Their spills were more likely to be from trying something new, such as skating backwards or a new dance move.

Music was typical skaters' music. Sometimes it would be a slow tune, like a waltz; other times it was fast and peppy for skate dancing. Everyone loved clicking their wheels to the music, kind of like tap-dancing on skates. And all the boys and girls enjoyed the couples skating. I wonder why?

The skating rink was the place where boys and girls gathered to meet kids from other schools. There was the typical flirting and laughter that all young people enjoy, but the real draw was the sound of those wheels on the floor.

Those who could dance to the music did and others simply enjoyed the round and round motion. Miss Polly knew how to mix up the sessions and would call for all to empty the floor to allow small children only, couples, or reverse skating. She kept the hours interesting by varying the music and skating activities. All the kids loved her, and she didn't hesitate to call down a rowdy boy or two when needed.

Going skating was the thing I did every Friday and/or Saturday night during high school. It was really the only place in Ardmore where young people could hang out and have fun without getting into trouble. Miss Polly didn't allow any misbehavior on the rink or outside if she knew about it. I think most kids respected her and her authority was never questioned to my knowledge. I spent many nights at Singing Wheels with my friends Aline and Wanda Holt and Aline's boyfriend, Tommy Hargrove. Yes, they were a couple in high school. Before I was in high school though, my baby sister and I frequented the rink every weekend with my older sister Marge.

One thing I remember about those early years was Bill Mitchell making fun of my feet because I was so small back then and my boots were about as big as me. I liked Bill, and I was so sorry to learn of his death in Korea during that war. He was a sweet guy. How sad he had to die young far away in a foreign country. I hope people in Ardmore remember him. He was one of the best.

The first year or so, I didn't own my own skates, but as any skater will tell you, owning your own is best. However, owning your own skates meant maintaining your wheels. One time, I was in a hurry to get on the floor— probably to flirt with one of the boys or talk with my friends, and forgot to check my wheels to make sure they were tight. As I was flying around the rink I rounded the end and was heading back toward the front when a back wheel came off my right skate. Ball bearings went flying all over the place, and I fell straight down on that hard floor. Talk about a sudden stop. Some kind person assisted me, and I had to get a new wheel put on. I never forgot after that. With ball bearings flying all over the rink, I'm sure there were others who wished I had checked my skates that night. It sometimes happened to others, so it wasn't just me thank heavens. Misery does love company.

Those were fun and very innocent days in Ardmore. As I have returned to Ardmore over and over as an adult, I have always been amazed that kids didn't seem interested in roller skating. It was wonderful exercise for all ages, and when I lived near Ardmore, I took my own kids there for exercise and fun. There have been times, as an adult, when I was tempted to pull on those skate boots one last time before father-time caught up with me. Alas, I didn't. Now Father-time has caught up with me, and the landmark is now gone. However, the memories of the skating rink are treasures to save and savor.

I can still hear "The Yellow Rose of Texas" playing as we skate danced our way around the rink. Some memories are such fun! I do often wonder though just how many miles I skated going in circles! Probably enough to have arrived in California by the time I was 18.

Going Home...

Thomas Wolfe wrote in his novel, *You Can't Go Home Again,* these words by the protagonist George Webber: "You can't go back home to your family, back home to your childhood ... back home to a young man's dreams of glory and of fame ... back home to places in the country, back home to the old forms and systems of things which once seemed everlasting but which are changing all the time — back home to the escapes of Time and Memory."

Though all of us have some place we call home, it really no longer exists. It is simply a memory. Going home always meant going back to the house in which I was raised; going back to see my parents, brothers and sisters, old friends, and to the way life as it was in the 1950s and '60s. I can no longer do that. It is literally impossible.

Both my parents are deceased as are my brothers and two of my sisters. Old friends, neighbors and other relatives have died. The home I knew where my mother planted beautiful flowers and my daddy kept the low mowed, the roadside banks neat, the house painted, and where a healthy garden, orchard and vineyard grew has been destroyed. It no longer exists, literally.

The home, where music was always in the air and delicious aromas emanated from my Mama's kitchen, is gone.

Gone are the family barbecues and holiday gatherings to which I often travelled thousands of miles to attend. Gone are my grandparents, aunts and uncles, and many others who filled my life.

The big locust tree where I often spread a handmade quilt and read to my heart's content, no longer exists-- chopped down by someone who cared little for its beckoning shade. This was my favorite dreaming place; and dream I did, of faraway places, exotic people and animals, of the husband I might one day marry and the children we might have.

Gone are the acres of apple trees with their sweet scent and the image of snow falling as the blossoms were shed and tiny apples began to form. Gone are the green apples we used to sneak when no one was watching. Gone are the many beautiful flowers my Mother planted and tended with such care. Now dug up, dead, and tossed into a junk heap.

Yes, I can still visit loved ones and friends when I return to my hometown, but as Wolfe wrote, there is no going back to the old ways and to your youthful dreams. As much as I would love to turn back the clock to a better time, it is impossible.

I realize that I'm growing older, and I see things so very different than I did at 20. But one thing I do remember is the way the average person lived in the 1950s and 60s. Remember we kids sang: First comes love, then comes marriage, then comes (insert name) with a baby carriage? Back then, a woman was shamed when she became pregnant outside marriage. The entire family was shamed. Today, it seems as if no one minds if a woman brings home several children by several different men or marries, divorces and remarries as do many Hollywood stars.

Another thing that has changed is that some young people no longer seem to care a great deal about elderly parents. Usually this is because the parents gave them everything their hearts desired when they were growing up—sacrificing to make things much easier and better for their children. As the parents age, they begin to reap their reward—selfish, self-centered adults who were once their coddled children.

I can't go home again to the countryside because the city is taking over all the rural areas. It used to be that small farms were the norm. Today, you have to have money to farm, and you have to have a lot of land to make a profit. Even the milk truck that served rural farmers as well as the creamery is gone.

I know that many of you who read this are saying you wouldn't change a thing—you love your cell phones that keep you tied to everyone who wants to reach out and touch someone—your homes on the lake or beach, the convenience of ordering on line, the wide array of products that are just a mouse click away. But if I could, I would gladly give up all those modern devices in order to go home again. Home to a society that moved a bit slower. Home to a society that really helped their neighbors. Home to a society that could trust its government (or so we thought) to always do what was right. Home to a society without illegal drugs. Home to a moral society. Yes, even home to a society that "clings to its guns and religion." But most of all, I'd gladly give up all modern inventions to go home once again to my family as they were many years ago—gathered together laughing, teasing and loving one another.

Yes, I'd gladly go home to that.

A Good Name Nowadays Is Hard to Find

When I was growing up, I often heard my folks talking about this one or the other in the neighborhood who had a bad reputation. Of course, they were usually conversations I was not supposed to hear, but sometimes they discussed them for the benefit of us children so that we'd know what happened if you really messed up and ruined your name.

You see in the South of my generation, a good name was worth more than gold; and we were often cautioned that our behavior not only reflected on us but on our family as well. We knew to take the straight and narrow path or find ourselves the subject of many a family discussion…ours and everyone else's within a 15 mile radius, perhaps a 50 mile radius if our actions warranted it.

I remember when we would hear about a lazy, town drunk that wouldn't work and take care of his family but spent his money on beer and whiskey. Other times it would be that a young girl was wild and that her actions were not good. Sometimes it was the fact someone had stolen something from another person and thus spoiled the name of the entire family.

Families held their names in high regard in those days unlike today when it seems a good name is often hard to find. Having a baby out of wedlock, being thrown into jail for public drunkenness, stealing and other sins were brought to our attention with the admonition that we should never do those things. Sometimes I thought that a person's name was more important than obeying God, but I've matured enough to know that someone who does have faith usually has a good name, so I guess they go hand in hand. Though at the time, I wasn't as aware of it as I am today.

I think most of us tried to live by the golden rule and the rules of our parents, but there were always those who slipped up. However, at that time few blatantly broke the rules and then pranced around as if they had been named homecoming queen…not in our neighborhood. If a girl became pregnant outside of marriage, it was kept it hidden until they quietly married. Today many young women do not think it unusual to be sleeping with someone before they are married or having a baby out of wedlock. Getting the cart before the horse was not optional for me and most of my generation. Today there is no shame in living with someone outside of marriage or even having a baby without the benefit of having a husband. Granted, I'm old; but I can't believe that even if I were 20 today I could have done that to my parents, and I certainly would never have done that to my grandparents. It was once shameful, and deep in my heart, I believe it still is no matter who does it.

I suppose we have Hollywood, television, celebrities and the devil to thank for the loose morals in this country. Think about it. How many of you now accept the fact that young people live together and have children without the thought of marriage. How many of you accept the homosexual lifestyle as right and proper? Personally, I find it rather sad that we have slipped into this low state, and that the BSA believes it is right and good to allow homosexual teens into their group when they are supposed to a Christian group. I don't know about your Bible, but mine still has the same words of admonition today as it did 50 or more years ago. I don't mean to preach because I'm not a preacher, but I will say that the family name has lost its luster in many a family.

I cannot even imagine having lived with my husband before marriage. I would have been so ashamed, and I could not have faced my parents, my aunts and uncles, my grandmother or my friends. I wonder how the younger generation can. What happened to marriage? Did I miss something along the way? When did it become passé to marry rather than just live together.

Yes, I'm old fashioned and believe the Bible is the Word of God. So, I'm assuming that in writing this article that I've offended some and stepped on the toes of many, but I do not apologize. I just hope that someday that this country will rid itself of the moral decay that is eating away at the fiber of the family. Then perhaps we could end abortions and broken families. If you doubt what immorality can do to a nation, pick up your dust-covered Bible and read what happened when the Israelites chose to "do what was right in their own eyes." God hasn't changed, and if you think he has, please refresh your memory by reading the good book.

If I could give advice to young women today it would be don't fall for a guy's sweet words until he is ready to back up those words with a marriage ceremony. Don't get pregnant outside of marriage and then opt for an abortion. One day you will rue the day you made either of these decisions. I don't think morals ever go out of fashion, but I feel that in today's culture that morals have taken a back seat and anything is allowed to go.

Ladies if you want a man to treat you with respect, make sure you respectful yourself first. You may think that it doesn't matter anymore, but I assure you that no one ever forgets all the wrong steps you take in life. Men...the same goes for you. Don't do anything that your grandmother would be ashamed of you for doing.

Where Did We Come From?

Well, of course, the first answer to that is that we came from God through Adam and Eve and on down the line. But if you were born in the Tennessee Valley and your parents and grandparents were born there as well and you are Welsh, Irish, Scottish or English descent, or even German, then you are probably a Celt, sometimes pronounced with a soft "c" as selt, but the preferred pronunciation is with the k sound, kelt. Of course, some of you may not be from this group. The South is diverse, as is the Tennessee Valley.

I don't claim to be a historian, but I do read a lot and have really delved into my own background. In having the Merrell DNA run, I discovered that we are definitely Celtic. Somewhere in time, my Mitochondrial DNA (MtDNA goes back through your mother and continues on back through the female side) comes from a female who lived in an area north of the Black Sea. This MtDNA Haplogroup, U5, has been estimated to be around 36,000 years old (though I don't know that I believe the number of years), and was among the first modern humans to populate Europe. Ancient DNA tests have shown that U5 was frequently found in hunter gathers in Europe before the development of agriculture.

Is it possible that you have hunter-gatherers in your family history? Yes, you probably do. One thing I'm sure of is that I'm probably 100% Celtic and proud of it. I don't even think that is a wild guess.

When I was asked in high school what I thought my race was, I always said Caucasian, and I was more right than I thought. Most of us think of ourselves as being European, but history tells me that there is a difference though I'm not sure I know how we differ. I have not done that much in-depth study on the subject, and I'm not sure I can separate the Cro Magnum from the Caucasians, but I'm assuming someone has. Many of us, who spring from European soil, however, are indeed Caucasian, and we are basically Celtic.

The Celts appear to have lived in Kazakhstan in an area called the Sea of Grass until late in the second millennium BC. They were a linguistic group, and contrary to what most believe, they had nothing to do with European inhabitants who were known as the Beaker folk (from Iberia) or Battle Axe people (possibly from Southern Russia). Instead, the Celts were related to the Urnfield people farther east in Circaesir. If you look at a map of the world, you'll find Kazakhstan way north of the Arabian Sea toward Russia.

The Urnfield people were a part of the Bronze Age, and they had a culture all their own. Their name derived from the fact they cremated their people's remains and interred them in urns. They inhabited a large area in central Europe, including Sicily, Scandinavia, France and Spain.

According to tradition, the Celts left the Sea of Grass after becoming unhappy with the Scythian confederacy. From all I've read, the Scythians were kind of like the elites in Washington today—throwing their weight around and using their power to their own advantage. So the Celts left the Sea of Grass and moved to what is now the Ukraine. The Sarmatians took over that area, but the Celts were firmly entrenched in central Europe by that time.

The Celts became very powerful in central Europe and dominated that area for several centuries since they were warrior types. They easily took over the area where the Faan's lived because as history indicates the Faan's were a peaceful people who didn't mind being dominated. Sounds like some people in America today.

The Celts moved south and west out of Central Europe, and brought with them their skill in metal work, trading and soldiering among others. Strictly speaking, the Celts probably should have been called Gaedheals because a similar people came by the Mediterranean Sea to Circaesya. It is recorded, perhaps it is a tradition not fact, that these migrants were descended from one Gaedheal Glas, son of Agnoman, who descended from

Magog, son of Japeth who was a son of Noah. Who knows if this is true, but it makes for good, spirited conversation. But the people have been known as Celtic throughout the centuries. In Wales, Ireland and Scotland the Celtic languages are different but similar.

The Celts were very capable people. In addition to their warrior talents which aided them in sacking Rome in 387 BC, they were skilled metal workers, built monasteries, created the beautiful artistic Book of Kells, and left their mark in several countries in that part of the world.

At the dawn of history, it is said that the Romans referred to the Celts in France as Gaul's, but even Caesar noted that they called themselves Celts and spoke their own language. Celtic societies have been portrayed as being divided into three groups: a warrior aristocracy; an intellectual class including professions such as druid, poet, jurist; and everyone else who apparently didn't fit the first two classes. In historical times, the offices of high and low kings in Ireland and Scotland were filled by election under the system of tanistry in which lands and titles were passed, but later conflicted with the feudal system of primogeniture in which the first son became the successor of titles and lands.

So, who are you, and where did you come from? That question cannot be answered with great assurance, but most likely you are at least part Celtic. I know my Celtic ancestry has been thoroughly proven through DNA. If you wish to have your own checked, it is relatively inexpensive to do through some of the genealogy sites on the internet.

The Declaration of Arbroath

I am including the Declaration of Arbroath which gave Scotland its Independence in 1320. It is in the format of a letter to Pope John XXII and is dated April 6, 1320 and was sealed by fifty-one magnates and nobles. It was drawn up at Arbroath Abby. The letter makes some important points. Namely that Scotland was always independent, that Edward I of England unjustly attacked Scotland and committed atrocities and that Robert the Bruce had to save Scotland from his attack. I'm including it here because many of us are of Scottish descent, and because it is a plea for liberty and rights of man, a right that our U.S. Constitution also gives us. If you wish to know more of its history, you can find writings on the Internet.

The Declaration translated in English follows:

The Declaration of Arbroath 1320

To the most Holy Father and Lord in Christ, the Lord John, by divine providence Supreme Pontiff of the Holy Roman and Universal Church, his humble and devout sons Duncan, Earl of Fife, Thomas Randolph, Earl of Moray, Lord of Man and of Annandale, Patrick Dunbar, Earl of March, Malise, Earl of Strathearn, Malcolm, Earl of Lennox, William, Earl of Ross, Magnus, Earl of Caithness and Orkney, and William, Earl of Sutherland; Walter, Steward of Scotland, William Soules, Butler of Scotland, James, Lord of Douglas, Roger Mowbray, David, Lord of Brechin, David Graham, Ingram Umfraville, John Menteith, guardian of the earldom of Menteith, Alexander Fraser, Gilbert Hay, Constable of Scotland, Robert Keith, Marischal of Scotland, Henry St Clair, John Graham, David Lindsay, William Oliphant, Patrick Graham, John Fenton, William Abernethy, David Wemyss, William Mushet, Fergus of Ardrossan, Eustace Maxwell, William Ramsay, William Mowat, Alan Murray, Donald Campbell, John Cameron, Reginald Cheyne, Alexander Seton, Andrew Leslie, and Alexander Straiton, and the other barons and freeholders and the whole community of the realm of Scotland send all manner of filial reverence, with devout kisses of his blessed feet.

Most Holy Father and Lord, we know and from the chronicles and books of the ancients we find that among other famous nations our own, the Scots, has been graced with widespread renown. They journeyed from Greater Scythia by way of the Tyrrhenian Sea and the Pillars of Hercules,

100

and dwelt for a long course of time in Spain among the most savage tribes, but nowhere could they be subdued by any race, however barbarous. Thence they came, twelve hundred years after the people of Israel crossed the Red Sea, to their home in the west where they still live today. The Britons they first drove out, the Picts they utterly destroyed, and, even though very often assailed by the Norwegians, the Danes and the English, they took possession of that home with many victories and untold efforts; and, as the historians of old time bear witness, they have held it free of all bondage ever since. In their kingdom there have reigned (stet) one hundred and thirteen kings of their own royal stock, the line unbroken a single foreigner. The high qualities and deserts of these people, were they not otherwise manifest, gain glory enough from this: that the King of kings and Lord of lords, our Lord Jesus Christ, after His Passion and Resurrection, called them, even though settled in the uttermost parts of the earth, almost the first to His most holy faith. Nor would He have them confirmed in that faith by merely anyone but by the first of His Apostles — by calling, though second or third in rank — the most gentle Saint Andrew, the Blessed Peter's brother, and desired him to keep them under his protection as their patron forever.

The Most Holy Fathers your predecessors gave careful heed to these things and bestowed many favours and numerous privileges on this same kingdom and people, as being the special charge of the Blessed Peter's brother. Thus our nation under their protection did indeed live in freedom and peace up to the time when that mighty prince the King of the English, Edward, the father of the one who reigns today, when our kingdom had no head and our people harboured no malice or treachery and were then unused to wars or invasions, came in the guise of a friend and ally to harass them as an enemy. The deeds of cruelty, massacre, violence, pillage, arson, imprisoning prelates, burning down monasteries, robbing and killing monks and nuns, and yet other outrages without number which he committed against our people, sparing neither age nor sex, religion nor rank, no one could describe nor fully imagine unless he had seen them with his own eyes.

But from these countless evils we have been set free, by the help of Him Who though He afflicts yet heals and restores, by our most tireless Prince, King and Lord, the Lord Robert. He, that his people and his heritage might be delivered out of the hands of our enemies, met toil and fatigue, hunger and peril, like another Macabaeus or Joshua and bore them cheerfully. Him, too, divine providence, his right of succession according to or laws and customs which we shall maintain to the death, and the due consent and assent of us all have made our Prince and King. To him, as to the man by whom salvation has been wrought unto our people, we are bound both by law and by his merits that our freedom may be still maintained, and by him, come what may, we mean to stand. Yet if he should give up what he has begun, and agree to make us or our kingdom subject to the King of England or the English, we should exert ourselves at once to drive him out as our enemy and a subverter of his own rights and ours, and make some other man who was well able to defend us our King; for, as long as but a hundred of us remain alive, never will we on any conditions be brought under English rule. It is in truth not for glory, nor riches, nor honours that we are fighting, but for freedom — for that alone, which no honest man gives up but with life itself.

Therefore it is, Reverend Father and Lord, that we beseech your Holiness with our most earnest prayers and suppliant hearts, inasmuch as you will in your sincerity and goodness consider all this, that, since with Him Whose vice-gerent on earth you are there is neither weighing nor distinction of Jew and Greek, Scotsman or Englishman, you will look with the eyes of a father on the troubles and privation brought by the English upon us and upon the Church of God. May it please you to admonish and exhort the King of the English, who ought to be satisfied with what belongs to him since England used once to be enough for seven kings or more, to leave us Scots in peace, who live in this poor little Scotland, beyond which there is no dwelling-place at all, and covet nothing but our own. We are sincerely willing to do anything for him, having regard to our condition that we can, to win peace for ourselves. This truly concerns you, Holy Father, since you see the savagery of the heathen raging against the Christians, as the sins of Christians have indeed deserved, and the frontiers of Christendom being pressed inward every day; and how much it will tarnish your Holiness's memory if (which God forbid) the Church suffers eclipse or scandal in any branch of it during your time, you must perceive. Then rouse the Christian princes who for false reasons pretend that they cannot go to help of the Holy Land because of wars they have on hand with their neighbours. The real reason that prevents them is that in making war on their smaller neighbours they find quicker profit and weaker resistance. But how cheerfully our Lord the King and we too would go there if the King of the English would leave us in peace, He from Whom nothing is hidden well knows; and we profess and declare it to you as the Vicar of Christ and to all Christendom. But if your Holiness puts too much faith in the tales the English tell and will not give sincere belief to all this, nor refrain from favouring them to our prejudice, then the slaughter of bodies, the perdition of souls, and all the other misfortunes that will follow, inflicted by them on us and by us on them, will, we believe, be surely laid by the Most High to your charge.

To conclude, we are and shall ever be, as far as duty calls us, ready to do your will in all things, as obedient sons to you as His Vicar; and to Him as the Supreme King and Judge we commit the maintenance of our cause, casting our cares upon Him and firmly trusting that He will inspire us with courage and bring our enemies to nought. May the Most High preserve you to his Holy Church in holiness and health and grant you length of days.

Given at the monastery of Arbroath in Scotland on the sixth day of the month of April in the year of grace thirteen hundred and twenty and the fifteenth year of the reign of our King aforesaid.

Endorsed: Letter directed to our Lord the Supreme Pontiff by the community of Scotland.

Additional names were written on some of the seal tags: Alexander Lamberton, Edward Keith, John Inchmartin, Thomas Menzies, John Durrant, Thomas Morham (and one illegible).

It isn't only to our founders in this country that we own our gratitude for developing our country around the constitution of this Republic. We also owe a debt of thanks to all those who have preceded us through history in fighting for the rights we now enjoy. It is important that we know our history, or as has been said before: "Those who cannot remember the past are condemned to repeat it." This was written by George Santayana, in Reason in Common Sense. Remember that our rights are not stationary as one would hope and believe. We have to be aware of the possibility of their loss each day less we lose them.

Scatter Shooting...

I sometimes use this heading for thoughts I have that just don't fit into any particular category. Under this heading, I'm including things such as snakes, spring cleaning, laundry day, and a conglomeration of thoughts. Even though they are separate entities, I hope that in them you'll get a glimpse of life in the 1940s and '50s.

Laundry Day came around once a week whether my mother was ready for it or not. With seven children and a husband to wash and iron for, it was a full day's job and during that time most everything else had to wait.

Mama's day began early in the morning when she would heat water to put in her electric wringer washing machine that sat on the back porch at one point, but was moved to other areas as needed. Unlike today's washers and dryers, this was an old tub washer with a wringer mechanism on top that was turned by hand to get the water out of the clothes. I don't know how many gallons of water it held, but I'm guessing at least 15 to 20. She had a hose to fill the tub with cold water, but the hot water had to be carted from the kitchen stove to the washer by hand.

Once the washer was filled, she added soap (often she used lye soap that she had made) and then added the white clothes or sheets first. These were washed, then the second load of colored clothes would go into the washer, and then the dark colors. Rinsing was done in a tub that sat by the washer and then the clothes were again run through the wringers to remove excess water.

There were times when my mother had to remove stains from the clothes before placing them in the washing machine. She would soak them first in soap and bleach, then she used a rub board to rub them on until the stains came out. Laundry day was very labor intensive in those years, and not something that most of us can even identify with since we have automatic washers that do all that labor for us.

When it was time to hang out the clothes to dry, we carried them by the tub full to the clothes lines and pinned them on with spring-type clothes pins. When it was hot and dry things dried fast and smelled heavenly when we brought them into the house. In fact, there is nothing like bed sheets that have been washed and dried in the sun. If you've never tried sleeping on sheets dried in the sun, you are missing a treat. On cold days, and it did get freezing cold in Middle Tennessee in the winter, we often brought in clothes from the line that had frozen stiff. They sometimes were dry enough to iron, but not always. Sometimes drying continued after they were taken from the line, but we only brought them in before they were dry when it was absolutely necessary.

Of course, the next day was ironing day. I remember actually using a flat iron to press clothes before we got an electric iron. I must have been rather young, but I do remember how we'd set them on the old wood burning cook stove in the kitchen to heat them, then pressing, reheating and pressing some more. They were hot, and you had to use great care in handling those irons. I don't know what became of the irons Mama had, but she had two of them until she died. I wanted one of them as a keepsake because I had used them, but I missed out somehow.

Clothing was often starched right after they were washed and before drying. In order to iron those starched jeans, shirts, dresses, etc., we had to sprinkle them using a homemade sprinkler that was made from a large soda bottle—probably a Coke or RC bottle since they were readily available. The sprinkler heads came from the local hardware store. As we sprinkled the clothes, usually on the kitchen table since it was the largest work surface, we'd roll them tightly to get the water to penetrate throughout the garment, then stash them in the fridge until we got them all done. After they sat for a little while, we'd take them out of the fridge, spread them out on the ironing board and try our best to keep from ironing more wrinkles into the wrinkly clothes.

When we got an electric iron, ironing was somewhat easier, but still very labor intensive since clothing was usually all cotton and sometimes pretty heavy weaves at that. Nobody ever wore clothing that wasn't starched and ironed. Of course, within 30 minutes of putting on a dress or shirt, they didn't look like it in the heat of summer.

Ladies if you never had the joy of washing and ironing as it was done in the 1940s, don't let me hear you complain about your automatic washers and driers, or how many loads you have to wash. You haven't lived a hard life unless you washed clothes as my mother did, and her mother before her. Before Mama bought a wringer washer, she washed clothes on a rub board, and had to carry the water from either a spring or a well to fill a huge caldron in which a fire was built around to heat it, then take the water to a tub and dilute it with cold water. That old copper kettle, as we called it, was black on the outside and copper on the inside, and it was huge, but it had a prominent place in our lives because that is where the water was heated in the 1930s and early 1940s. No wonder my mother was never overweight. She worked from sun up to bedtime 6-7 days per week, and yet lived to be 88 years old. So, please don't complain about your laundry loads. They just don't compare.

*****

A memory I've carried with me since I was about 7 years old is as fresh in my mind today as it was back in 1943 or '44. It is of me standing on the front porch of our house, with my hands shielding my eyes, peering at my mother at the edge of the woods, a good football field away, with a hoe in her hand. She was there trying to kill two huge black snakes that had just scared the daylights out of me.

Mama and I had walked down to the woods to pick up sticks for kindling so that she could use them to start a fire to burn trash. As we walked near the old sorghum cane pommie pile, that is the pulp that is left after the juice has been squeezed out, I spotted the snakes. Since Daddy had made molasses for several years during sorghum cane harvest time, there was always a huge pile of pommies that no doubt rodents discovered and lived in, thus enticing snakes to their feast.

No matter where I wander, no matter where I roam, I've always found snakes when no one else knew they were within 10 miles. I attract the snakes or they attract me, I'm not sure which. Anyway, the minute I saw them, I dropped the few sticks I had been carrying and was on the porch before Mama could turn around. Fortunately, she had a hoe with her, and she took care of those two huge snakes. In my mind's eye, they always appear to be about 8 feet long and 5 inches around, but were more likely much smaller than that. To a small kid, they looked gigantic. Snakes have been the bane of my existence. Although I love the country, I knew from the time I was a little girl that I didn't want to live among snakes. So, what did I do when I grew up? I moved to the Elkmont Rural Village in Elkmont, AL and bought a house and lot. About two years after moving there, I learned from my old friend Joe Evans that in his youth, they had called that hill where ERV was built rattlesnake hill, and believe me, there were rattle snakes there, along with copper heads, and all other kinds of creatures. I was a pretty nervous Nellie living out there, but I soon learned to cope with the wild life and loved the peace I found from living close to nature.

I did not come to terms with snakes shedding their skins in my garage, and I used every tactic known to man to keep them out of my garage. I never, ever stepped foot in that garage unless I turned on lights. Unlike Eve I didn't want anything to do with snakes, and I still don't. Just driving alone in the car, I'll automatically lift my feet when I see a snake in the road. They send cold chills over me to this day.

*****

Another snake story is also stuck in my memory. This one after I was married. On our delayed honeymoon in April 1960, we were heading down to see Bob's mother and sister in West Palm Beach, FL and then on to Key West. Along the way, we stopped in Silver Springs, and I enjoyed almost all of the visit there, but not the outdoor reptile show Bob wanted to stop and see. I made him sit way back in the audience just in case one of those snakes got loose, but that didn't save me.

The guy showed a number of snakes, all very good sized ones, and then he brought out a big old black snake. For someone who was scared to death of snakes, that snake looked as if it was 20 feet long and continuously wrapping itself around his arms. He said something to the effect that the snake wasn't poisonous, but I was thinking, that doesn't make any difference to me. Just running across one would probably give me a heart attack.

Now my sweet husband, who knew I was terrified of snakes, was sitting alongside me taking in the demonstration, and I had no idea that he would put my life in jeopardy. He did. This snake handler said he wanted someone to come up to the stage and hold the snake. I cringed, but I knew I would never volunteer for that. But, my dear husband, quietly put his hand behind my back, held it over my head and pointed to me. That guy called me up front, and I refused to go. Then he and my husband together insisted I go. The only way I could get out of it was a quick divorce, and I wasn't in Reno or Las Vegas. So with great reservations, I went to the stage, with that old snake curling around his arms trying to get loose.

The snake handler said which end do you want to hold? I said neither. He said you have to hold one or the other. So I finally told him I'd hold the tail end, but only if he held the head a long way away from me. I touched the tail and my skin started crawling. He said get a firm hold. So weak and trembling, there I stood with the tail of a snake in my hand. I held that tail for what seemed like hours, but was probably 30 seconds, and he said, now I want you to hold this end also. I said, no, absolutely not. He said if you don't, I'm going to drop the end of the snake. Well...I figured that holding the snake behind the head would be preferable to having it trying to crawl up my leg, so I took hold of it and Bob snapped my picture. I don't think I held it long. I vaguely recall saying, here take this thing or I'm going to throw it down. He did, and I hightailed it off that stage to the sound of a lot of giggles, one guffaw (from you know who) and loud applause.

I was so mad at my husband I could barely speak to him. Believe me I made him pay for that little trick. I told his Mother when I got to West Palm Beach. She threatened him within an inch of his life for scaring me to death, but he just chuckled, and I knew if he had the opportunity he would do that again. I never gave him a chance. That was my last snake show.

*****

There is a tale in our family of one of our Reed forefathers who ran the Red House Inn in Rowan County, NC. The first story has to do with George Washington staying there as he passed through NC once, and it is possible that story is true. However, the story that always makes all of us laugh is the one where he had company come and stay for a lengthy visit.

George Reed apparently was a good businessman and farmer, and he really did have a mind of his own. It seems these friends or relatives had come to visit and had long overstayed their welcome. He wanted them to leave, but in true Southern fashion, he didn't want to ask them to leave. I suppose strong hints were OK, but they apparently didn't take the bait.

Since it was in the winter, he decided the best way to get rid of them was to make them uncomfortable. So, he allowed the temperature in the house to get down so low that everyone was about to freeze and his company decided they needed to move on.

My great-great-great-granddaddy George Reed "froze them out." Once when I was visiting my nephew in Rolla, MO in the dead of summer, he had every ceiling fan on in his house and the air conditioning turned so low

I almost froze. I accused him of trying to get rid of me as old George did his overstaying guest. He just laughed and said, he wasn't cold. Of course, my nephew wasn't really trying to get rid of us…or was he? We'll never know. It is fun to tease about it though.

Another George Reed story. There were three George Reeds in a row, but this is the story about the one above. George donated land for the Baptist Church at Reeds Cross Roads, NC along with the cemetery, and was a frequent benefactor of the church. They often came to him once for help, and once they asked him to put a new roof on the church. He agreed to do so. Since George liked to drink a little whiskey, sometime later the church fathers asked him to quit drinking. He told them that if they didn't like his drinking, he'd just take his roof and go elsewhere. They left him alone and took his money, which no doubt was a wise decision on their part. He sounded like someone who didn't mince words. Wish I could have known him.

******

Mama used to take us to revivals in Ardmore during the summer. She enjoyed church, so she'd make us all get cleaned up and go to church. One summer she decided to go when her sister Geneva and husband, Johnny Procak, were visiting from Yonkers, NY. Johnny was just a kid at heart, and we always loved him and his Yonkers brogue. While visiting with them at my Grandmother's, we all decided to go to the local Church of Christ for the revival meeting that night.

It was the dog days of summer, and this small church was filled to capacity. The weather was about as hot as you have ever seen an August night, and everyone in the church was sweating and fanning with funeral home fans.

Now, the preacher may have thought we were all sweating listening to his hell fire and damnation sermon, but most were just hot from the weather.

Of course, since Johnny was every kid's buddy, I sat on one side of him with his wife and my mother on the other. My sister Faye was there too, but I can't recall exactly where she was sitting, but probably by Mama.

Johnny and I had been sitting quietly, and that was unusual, but a necessity in church, with Mama so close by. But soon, as the preacher was yelling that some of us were going to hell, a big horse fly flew into the church through one of the open windows or door, and lit on the head of the bald headed man in the pew in front of us. It sat on this man's head for a few minutes, apparently lapping up the salty sweat, and the man didn't move. Soon, Johnny was poking me and giggling, while pointing at the fly on the glistening head and that got me going. I cannot stop laughing if someone causes me to start, and even though I knew I was going to be in trouble, I snickered (quietly) and squirmed around. Pretty soon, the fly flew away without the man ever acknowledging it had been there, and I finally got my giggles under control. But not soon enough!

Mama spotted me and shook her finger at me. If she had been sitting close enough, she'd have pinched me, but she wasn't. But I knew I was not going to escape her punishment.. She gave me a licking as we walked back to grandma's house that night, and threatened me with hell fire and brimstone if I ever did it again. OK…she didn't say exactly that, but I got the idea. She was going to make my life pretty uncomfortable if I ever acted up in church again. Fortunately, for me, she never did catch me acting up, but I emphasize the word "catch." Kids always do things to push the limits of their boundaries, and I sometimes did. I do not recommend it if you have a strict mother as I had.

*****

Everywhere I've lived, I've found good friends. Some of my friends I've had since elementary school. Others have been added as I've moved from place to place, but they are all important to me. I treasure my friends, and I hope they know how special they are to me.

112

One friend who was a neighbor in Elkmont Rural Village became very close to me during our years there together. I remember meeting this talented woman and immediately thinking of how nice she was. Always a good Christian woman, Pat was not a person to put on airs. She was who she was, and I liked that about her. She had two pet desert turtles that lived in their house and two beautiful golden retrievers, along with her husband and three daughters. She was a good cook, an excellent organist and choir director, and she always filled her home with family and friends.

The reason I tell about Pat is that she invited me to attend some shindig at the Athens Country Club one day, and I thought it would be fun to go since I did enjoy her company. So, we traveled down to the club house, and before going into the meeting area, we stopped by the bathroom. As she started to put her keys in her pocket, she realized that her culottes were on backwards. Was she embarrassed? No. She simply stepped into a stall, removed them and put them on the correct way. We had a good laugh out of it, and I've always told her since then that I knew the minute I saw that her culottes were on backwards that she would be my friend. She was and still is.

Pat is a cancer survivor, and I'm so grateful that we're still friends though we live 800 miles apart. I love the Chacon family. They are generous, loving and kind people. The world needs more like them.

Revivals in the South

I have lived all across this country, and I've yet to find anyplace outside the South that has so many revivals. There must be something inherent in our Southern culture that requires us to need reviving a couple times each year. We were really bad or really good—far be it from me to give an answer to that.

The church of my childhood was a Southern Baptist Church, and I can assure you that services were held twice on Sunday and once in the middle of the week, yet people still needed that twice a year reviving that only an out of town preacher could provide. I remember going to the revivals in the summer when the windows were open and without screens. We used a funeral parlor fan to keep cool. It didn't help much, but it did give you something handy to swat the bugs with that came in to hear the preacher's message each night. We weren't the only ones battling the heat and bugs. The preacher was in a more precarious position because bugs could try to crawl into his ears, up his nose or in his mouth. I don't think I ever saw a preacher stop to get a bug out of any of his cavities, but they sure did work up a sweat talking about how hot it was going to be in hell, and I for one believed him since it was hot sitting in church.

Regular attendance at revivals was a way of life. We often had to walk to get to church, but my Mama would clean us all up, slick down my brother's hair and get the tangles out of mine and my sister's so we would be presentable at church. Kids who go to Catholic, Lutheran and Episcopal Churches never get to hear the hellfire and damnation sermons I heard as a child; therefore, they have little fear of the Lord's wrath. However, there were none of these churches in our immediate area, so all my friends were Baptist, Methodist or Church of Christ, and it kept us mostly on the straight and narrow path. I say mostly, because there isn't a child born that is perfect, and we certainly weren't. However if those liturgical churches that serve wine for communion had heard the preacher expound on the sins caused by alcohol, they might have avoided going to the communion rail. I know I would have.

As a kid, I enjoyed the revivals and Bible School. But as I approached my 10th year, there were several older ladies in the church who felt it was their mission in life to save my soul. I don't know why they didn't believe that God was quite capable of accomplishing that task without their help, but they didn't seem to think so.

Everything went smoothly during the first part of revival week. We sang many old hymns and listened to good, instructive sermons, prayed and heard the preacher each night giving the altar call. But about mid-week, if you hadn't made your way down front to the altar and confessed your sins to the preacher, one or the other of those ladies would single you out and start working on you. It never failed. You could see it coming. First, you'd see their heads turning during the invitation with all eyes directed on one of us sinners. Sitting in the choir, they would sing verse after verse of "Just as I am" staring directly at one of us. It was a different one each night that gained this honor. If you didn't make a move to go down front, you knew you'd live to regret it. But there are some things that simply can't be rushed. Salvation is one of those.

I often suspected these ladies informed the preacher which of us kids was the most stubborn or tardy about confessing our sins and asking forgiveness. Because he, too, would often have a gleam in his eye as the singing got underway, and if no one budged when the song was finished, we'd sing the last verse over and over again. On occasion, the preacher would say, "With every eye closed and every head bowed, I want you to raise your hand if you need Jesus in your life or need praying for tonight." I never raised my hand because I knew that some "sinner" would be peeping, and I didn't think it was any of their business.

We often did sing those verses over and over again giving the sinner a lot of time to make up his mind, but not always. There were times when

116

someone who was already a Christian would go forward and rededicate his or her life, and that took the heat off the rest of us recalcitrant individuals. However, we knew the "missionary ladies" would be hurrying outside after the meeting to waylay us.

Now I'm not saying that it was wrong for these nice ladies to want us to confess our sins and be saved. I'm just saying that sometimes something so very personal is best left to the individual to make that decision themselves. Granted most of us young kids didn't know how to make decisions, but we were capable of learning. That didn't stop the ladies who felt it their duty as upstanding ladies of the church to cajole us into doing what they wanted.

Of course, being the kids we were, as soon as the preacher ended the service with an Amen, we were out the door. But I think those little ladies wore track shoes because they caught up with us outside. There they would plea with you to turn your life over to the Lord and ask you to be baptized. This would go on each night until revival was over or we'd given in and gone to the altar.

I won't say that many children weren't saved during these revivals. I'm saying that some were pushed into doing something they might not have been really sure about. As my 12th birthday approached, I knew I was pushing my luck with the ladies, so that August during the revival meeting, I really listened to what the preacher was telling us. I suppose, much to the little ladies' surprise, I went forward one night claiming the salvation that Christ so willing died on the cross to give me. No, I didn't do it because I knew the ladies were going to be after me again. I did it because at some time during the revival I realized what Jesus had done for me, and I wanted to be a part of his kingdom. So, even though they thought they had worked their magic on me for years and converted me, alas it was not they who persuaded me to take the walk. It was the Word itself. Too bad I never told them, but then it might have ruined their day. They did mean well, I'm sure.

Revivals aren't just held in the Baptist Church, they are the norm in most Protestant churches in the south, except for the liturgical churches mentioned before. We had a neighbor who was also a close friend who was a member of another church, but she did so enjoy going to the Holiness Church revivals. Every summer, she'd get her husband to take her down to Ardmore to one of the Holiness tent revivals that were held for a week.

We sometimes drove past where the revival was being held, but not for the purpose of seeing what was going on. Daddy didn't think that was a nice thing to do. However, I tried to get a good look at what was happening in that tent, but I never saw anything out of the ordinary. I had to depend on my neighbor for a description, and she was always willing to share.

She would tell us about the music and singing that put everyone into frenzy, then how the men and women would come under the "spell" of the Holy Spirit. I remember her telling us about the ladies rolling in the floor and their dresses coming up above their knees. In the 1950s, women still wore calf length dresses, so showing their knees was simply not proper in church. She said the tops of their stockings were often showing, but I don't know if they got any higher. She may have elaborated a bit on the meeting just to entertain us, but I suspect there was a grain of truth in her descriptions. Perhaps fortunately, I never got to see for myself. That was one thing my folks prohibited us from doing—that is going to a church to just see what was going on. My folks loved to have fun, but that was strictly off limits. Now I can understand why.

I remember sitting in church one hot summer night trying to listen to the sermon, but I was being distracted by my cousin Jackie Dale Ferguson who sat beside me. Jackie was a few years younger than me, but he had such an outgoing personality that he was fun to be around regardless of his age. He could never totally behave himself as a kid, and he began making wise cracks under his breath accompanied by funny faces. I couldn't help laughing at his antics, and that got me in trouble. I didn't know that Daddy had gone outside where it was cooler to listen to the sermon. Since it was nighttime, we couldn't see out, but he could see in through the open windows. He apparently had a good view of Jackie and me. When I got in the car that night, Daddy was waiting for me, and I can assure you that from that day on I tried to avoid the very appearance of evil when I was in church. Daddy didn't spank. He just let me know in no uncertain terms that my conduct was not appropriate. I suspect Jackie got called for his conduct as well, and that he and I both got F's in deportment that night. Jackie in now deceased. He was a sweet young man, and such a bright spirit. No doubt he entertains folks in heaven.

As I look back on my childhood, I realize how much going to church, attending revivals and Bible school shaped my life. Not only were the seeds of faith planted then, but also respect for my elders, love of my country and my fellowman. There were so many wonderful men and women in our little country church who influenced my life, even the sweet ladies I called the churches missionaries earlier. They were all honest, hard-working farmers who lived exemplary lives. They were wonderful examples to all of us who grew up in Cash Point Baptist Church, and I thank the Lord for placing me in their midst.

After I grew up and married, I became a member of the Lutheran Church – Missouri Synod because that was my husband's faith, and we wanted to worship together. There are many similarities between the two churches; though both probably would not admit it. They both believe that the Bible is the inspired word of God without exception. They both believe in Baptism though not necessarily in the same form. They both teach and preach the Law and the Gospel and while one has a more formal worship than the other, the sermons and Bible teachings are Bible based. They both believe there is only one path, and that is through Christ. One thing that is different is the Lutheran's hymns are different. Most are based directly on the Psalms, and most were written in the 1500-1800s. Seldom will you hear gospel songs in a traditional Lutheran Church, but that is changing a bit in the 21st century. I used to tease my husband and say that the reason he couldn't sing was that the Lutheran songs only had two notes. Of course, that isn't true, but their songs for the most part are not typical songs that are sung in the Baptist or Methodist Churches. I find they are not as melodious, but what can I say? I love the music of the Baptist, Methodist and Presbyterian Churches.

There have been times when I'd love to stand up in the Lutheran Church and belt out a spiritual song, but with my singing voice it would sound more like screeching and I'd be excommunicated. Unfortunately, I barely make a joyful noise anymore. It has never stopped me from tying I must admit.

Note: I hope no one thinks I'm making fun of revivals. I have a very strong Christian faith that stems from the things I learned as child. I fully believe in a resurrected Christ. I believe that God created the world, and that the Holy Spirit exists and does teach and bring us comfort. That is something I know up close and personal. And with that said, I hope that the way I live my life proves that point.

Newspapers, Politicians and Funny Things

I've spent many years writing for newspapers, and I've always said if I had a nickel for every word I'd written, I'd be a millionaire. However, as anyone who has ever worked for a newspaper knows, the pay is low, the hours are long, and you always work on holidays. While everyone else was enjoying a family day on July 4th, Labor Day or almost any holiday except Christmas and Thanksgiving, I was usually on duty. That part wasn't fun, but I confess that I have printers ink in my veins, and I do not know how to rid myself of it. I've tried bleach, lye, and non-chlorine bleach, but I still keep putting words on paper. By the way, I am kidding about the bleaches and lye so do not try it. But I'm not kidding about the fact that I often feel if I don't write down my thoughts my head will explode. So to avoid an explosion that would be messy and useless, I write.

I've had some interesting things happen through the years. When I worked on a daily newspaper, I typically was assigned to cover government and/or education as those were my specialties. On a weekly, I did whatever needed doing, sometimes cleaning up the floor around the paste-up boards where we did all that cutting and pasting by hand. Now it is done by computer and so much easier and cleaner.

Since I covered county and local government, I was often brought into the publisher's office to meet local, county or state politicians. I knew going in that I was going to be asked to paint a pretty picture of this politician who, like you and I, had feet of clay.

I remember once heading into my cigar-smoking-publisher's office to meet one of his political want-a-be's and finding that I already knew the gentlemen in question. In fact, he was a neighbor. I asked to be excused from that project, but a few years later I served as his campaign chairman for public office. In between that first official meeting and my work on his campaign, he had run for office and won. I realized then that he was the type candidate I could support, so I did not hesitate to work for his election to another office. But I have to confess, he was one of the few that I had much faith in who came into the office seeking publicity. I really don't know what my publisher gained from treating these people so well. There were some that I simply could not support, and I made sure my boss knew so he'd ask someone else to write their stories. I know how to write, and I know how to interview; but I don't know how to lie about someone I don't trust. My boss knew that.

In one small town where I was working on a newspaper, there were a couple of bank vice-presidents who worked at competing banks. I received phone calls from each of them at least twice a week. It was usually a request for something to be placed in the paper, but it always entailed putting a picture of them in the paper along with an article.

One of these ladies was younger and much better looking than the other. Because of that, she photographed well. The other lady did not take good photos, and every time a good photo of the first lady ran, she'd call and complain that we were playing favorites and not using her best photo. That was not true, but she would not believe it. I so often wanted to tell her that we worked with what we had, but while I wasn't afraid of my cigar-smoking boss, I didn't want to bring down his wrath unnecessarily. So I didn't express my opinion, but simply told her we'd try to do better.

Another time, I had a lady that would call me for the least little thing to get her photo in the paper. I've never understood why someone really wanted to get their name or photo in the paper. Maybe that is because I had to use a by-line on everything I wrote, and it just didn't seem glamorous to me. To this middle aged woman, however, it must have been what she lived for because I got calls at least once or twice a week.

She belonged to some sort of homemakers organization or garden club...can't remember which, but she would call me if she was baking bread and had a beautiful loaf that everyone needed to see, or had a hanging basket that was just bursting with blooms that needed to be in the paper...accompanied by her face as well.

I put up with that for about a year and a half, and I finally went in and told my publisher that if I was asked to make another photo and write a cutline (most of you refer to them as captions) for it, I was going to scream and run outside in the street naked. I think he thought I might do that because he had the receptionist direct her calls to someone who would take a message and lose it. I think she got the message.

I never heard from her after that, but I can assure you, her picture ended up on the bottom of bird cages for months since it was printed regularly.

Once I had a mayor politely tell me that I could leave the city council meeting I was covering. I was the only reporter there, and he had apparently done this to reporters before. I sat there a minute and he just sat and looked at me, and I finally said, I don't think you can ask me to leave unless you're going to have an executive meeting. He said, oh, the meeting is over. Well, since I didn't want to get into a cuss-fight or a fist-fight, I picked up my purse and notebook and left. He had not closed the meeting, and they continued to meet while I sat outside for at least 30 minutes waiting to see when they all left.

The next morning I went into my publisher's office and told him what happened. It really annoyed him since the Sunshine law states that all official meetings of any public body is open to the public unless they are discussing a person's character...not job performance, that is public knowledge, but character, meaning integrity, honor, reputation, etc. So, he told me to write up the story starting with the fact I was told to leave, and I did. That afternoon, the newspaper was in the mayor's hands, and my publisher received a call. After a quick dressing down by my boss, the mayor wrote a letter to the editor for the next day's paper, which went on the front pay since that is where the first story was placed, apologizing to me and to the public. I will say that from that day on, this mayor never attempted to pull a stunt like that because my boss wasn't afraid to call a spade a spade.

Another time, a different mayor called and told my boss he'd read my article and that he thought we were at two separate meetings. I always took copious notes, and I always had someone within who attended the same meetings that I made friends with to make sure I had backup. So when my boss called me in, I was prepared with my notes and told him I could get someone to vouch for me that the facts as written were accurate. He asked me to have this person call him, and I did (it was a councilman, by the way), and he verified my story. So, this mayor tucked his tail and never gave me any trouble after that. Again my boss wasn't afraid to stand up for his employee.

I've had to butt heads with a lot of politicians during my career as a reporter, but I don't back down when I'm right. They may not like me, but I wasn't there to win a popularity contest. Those who did their jobs and didn't lie to the public always respected me, and I've had numerous awards for my work. Those who were trying to hide something from the public didn't like me reporting on their meetings because I never lied. I can honestly say that I never deliberately went after someone to make them look badly or to put words in their mouths that they didn't say. But I did report the facts as presented without editorializing in my article, and I let the chips fall where they may. As one of my editors told me once, "You don't have to make them look bad. They make themselves look bad when they open their mouths." So often true.

I have made mistakes in reporting, and I'm the first to admit it. Once I was asked to do a brief front page article on a Savings and Loan. The information presented to me was their earnings report for the quarter with back up details. Since I was typing the article on a typesetter (this was before computer keyboards by the way, but similar), I could only see 13 characters at a time. When I was writing about their gross earnings for the quarter, I inadvertently left off about three zeros. Instead of writing the S&L had gross earnings of $1,300,000; it became $1,300. Proofreaders didn't catch it and neither did I. Of course the president called the office the next day, and asked for a re-write with the proper numbers. I was given the job since I had made the mistake, and as always, wherever the story was placed originally in that newspaper, the correction was placed in the same spot the next day.

When my boss told me what happened, I knew immediately because I had been interrupted when I was typing the figures and just forgot that I didn't finish the number and went on to the sentence. So, I got a chuckle out of it, and I sat down at my typesetter and wrote my correction. I made a joke of it. I said, that in one swift keystroke I had robbed the S&L of almost $300,000 dollars—something that Bonnie and Clyde couldn't have accomplished without getting shot. Then I went on to give the actual figures that should have been reported.

The next morning when I came in, my boss called me in and laughingly said; well you made ole "Jim" very happy yesterday. I said, Oh? Yes, my boss said, your tongue in cheek correction was the talk of everyone in town. Best advertisement he could have gotten. So, the president was happy, my boss was happy, and I had a good laugh as well. That's what started me writing about funny happenings in a column. See, you never waste a good opportunity to get noticed or make someone laugh. I kind of liked that and continued it for years.

I did take my job seriously, and I enjoyed it immensely. I spent many years covering meetings, taking photos, interviewing people for stories, and I enjoyed it all. I was born for this type work and there were times I enjoyed it so much I'd have paid them to let me work. I've always said that when you are in a field of work that is suited to you, it isn't work. It is more like playing. You're doing your job and doing your best, but it is fun.

I remember visiting in the home of a little lady who was well over a hundred to interview her. She was so bright and articulate, could see well and hear well so she was just a joy to interview. An interview that should not have lasted more than an hour lasted at least two because I was enjoying hearing her stories.

Another time, I interviewed one of the first generation German-Americans whose father and uncles came to Limestone County, AL in the 1800s to help build a railroad. This gentleman was quite elderly, but I don't remember exactly how old. He had gone to the only Lutheran Church in the county when he grew up, (St. Paul's Lutheran Church) so I was fascinated with the church's history. It seems they only spoke German at that church because all who attended were new to America. As their children grew up and went to school in the county, they began to marry non-Germans who didn't speak the language. So the church basically died due to the language barrier when the first generation of kids became immersed in the American culture and English language. For the parents of that generation, I'm sure it was a bitter/sweet experience, but truthfully that is the way it should be. Remember your heritage, but merge into your new home's culture so that you become united. Unfortunately it doesn't seem to happen that way anymore. A visit to any large city will prove that point.

Another interview I did was also memorable, but not because it was such a pleasant interview. Well, the person was OK. It was the circumstances.

I was asked to do interviews of various people who were teaching continuing education courses in the town where I lived. So, I set up the interview one hot May morning and trekked across town to do my job.

As I approached the door, I could hear dogs and cats making a racket in the house, and when she opened the door, I almost lost my breakfast from hours before. There was such a stench coming from inside that woman's house that I could barely stand it. I've always had a "nose" for odors, and I suffered while in her house.

The lady was well educated and intelligent. She not only played musical instruments well, but she also made dulcimers. I was interested in the class she was going to be teaching, but I did that interview in about a third the time I would have taken due to the stench. I think all her cats peed in the house, and I'm sure the dogs needed baths. When she offered me a cup of tea; I declined. There was no way I could have sipped tea. I told her I had another appointment and had to rush. I didn't lie. I had to go home and take a shower. That's how bad I smelled after 20 minutes there. I promised myself never do another interview about dulcimers. I didn't. I still have a miniature pendant of one she gave me. I keep it to mind myself never to do that again.

These were just a few of many memorable interviews I did. I did not keep copies of the articles or my notes, and I'm sorry I didn't. They were such interesting people with so many stories to tell.

I took so many photos of groups and civic events that I often said that when I walked into a room with a camera in my hand, everyone backed up against a wall and smiled. It was almost the truth and only a bit of an exaggeration. When I took photos, I wanted the people lined up by height and in orderly rows. You'd be surprised how short people like to stand behind taller ones. I always would say, if you can't see my camera, I can't see you, so move so that your face is in between the face of the two people in the row in front of you. That worked sometimes, but not always. Unfortunately, I did not have a digital camera back then, so I would have to take three shots to make sure that the only photo usable did not have someone with crossed eyes, hair hanging in front of their nose or sprouting something from the back of their head...that happens if you don't have a simple background. Usually my biggest problem was getting shots of kids who wanted to giggle and talk while I was trying to capture their cute faces.

The only time I was ever really angry was when a woman from a prestigious organization, of which I was a member but not of her group, kept telling me how she wanted pictures of about 30 kids taken. I listened to her for a while, put up with her changing kids around to suit herself (usually putting a favorite kid in front and blocking a smaller one), and using my time for no purpose.

I finally had enough of her, and I politely asked her if she would mind sitting at a table nearby and letting me set up my shots. Now handling that many kids is difficult because they all want to squirm and squint, say something dumb or just act up. But I finally got their photos along with others I needed and started to leave. As I was going out the door this woman said to someone as I was passing, "That old woman from _____, made me so mad. She acted as if it was her pictures." I stopped and looked at her, and I said, "This old woman (and I was younger than her by far) happened to be doing the job she was sent to do, and my job is to get the best photos I can of those kids. They are the newspaper's pictures." I didn't smile or say anything else. But she looked as if she had swallowed a dead rat.

I did tell my boss about the incident, and I don't think any of her photos ever made the newspaper, but that was not my responsibility, and I didn't worry about it. I hated it because of the kids, but she really was being bitchy. There are some people who always want to tell a reporter or photographer how to do their jobs. If they truly know what they are doing that is one thing, but if they are just being controlling that is a horse of a different color. When a newspaper sends someone out for photos, they want photos that look well in their paper. So please, if you're reading this, offer to help if it appears needed but allow the employee to do the job.

While writing for a local paper, I began writing a weekly column, and I occasionally still write an article for them. Mostly, my articles were just fun things that happened to me, but at times they were serious as well. I remember once telling everyone about a mishap with my blender and hot potato soup, and I've never lived that one down. I confess that I was a mess with potato soup in my hair, all over my clothes; counter, cabinets and even the ceiling. No, I wasn't so stupid that I didn't put the lid on the blender. But try blending hot soup, and I guarantee you that unless the lid is weighted down by a 2,000 pound elephant, it is going to explode all over the place. Never blend hot soup! I think they could make bombs with blenders and hot soup, but forget I said that. I don't want anyone trying it.

I often told about my foibles in my columns. I've had people tell me that even though they didn't know me that they knew all about me. I don't mean to disappoint anyone, but there are times when I made up silly stories just to entertain others, and like a comedian on the stage, I didn't mind making fun of myself if it would make someone else laugh. As anyone who knows me can tell you, I'm someone who can laugh at my own stupidity, and as long as you laugh along with me, I'm happy. However, I'm really a pretty reserved person. So don't let my writing fool you too much. But if I can cause you to forget your own problems for a few minutes, that is my goal. I did warn people there were times I would write the truth about myself and other times I wouldn't. A disclaimer, if you will. It worked for me, but I'm not sure it worked for everyone.

I took a test drive in the corporate world for a few years. I was still mostly writing, but it was far more formal and stressful. I remember once walking into a meeting thinking that I was just a couple minutes early and sitting down in the meeting only to be met with strange looks. I quickly grasped that it was an ongoing meeting. So I got up and hightailed it out to the outer office to find out what was going on. I didn't realize that, but since some of the key players were the same as involved in my meeting, I thought they were just chatting. After that I learned that the old saying "fools rush in where angels fear to tread" is a good one to remember. No one ever said anything to me about my error, but I really was embarrassed. My "sin" was that I have always adhered to the "be on time" rule, and I was on time. It's just there were laggards ahead of me. I have often wished I wasn't so addicted to obeying rules, but I confess that I am. If the speed limit says 45, then I try to keep my speed at 45. I don't take laws to be suggestions. If it says thou shalt not smoke in this establishment, even if I were a smoker and dying for a cigarette, I'd obey the law. I'm not sure if it comes from the way I was raised, or whether I was just born with that inclination. There have only been a few times when I had the urge to break the law, but that was in my very young days when I was young and dumb and my brain hadn't completely developed. Even then I had a nagging conscious that stayed with me, and I never did anything that was bad. Mostly I just thought about it. According to the Bible, that might be the same thing except no one ever gave me a ticket for thinking. At least, not yet!

In my early working career, I worked for the Department of Army for several years. It was there that I found so many life-long friends. One of those friends was Barbara Atkins Reed. I met Barbara while I was attending school in Huntsville, and we remained friends until her death in 2004. When I met Barbara, she was a Gospel DJ in Huntsville, WBHP radio, as I recall; and we had so much in common that we could always pick up where we left off even if we didn't see one another for several years. That was because I was always moving across the country. Anyway, Barbara was extremely bright, and she came to Redstone Arsenal and worked in the Judge Advocate's office (for a bunch of military lawyers). She had a fun spirit, and since she worked just down the street from where I did in the old Redstone headquarters building, we often had lunch together. I never had the guys swarming the table when I was alone, but when blond, petite Barbara sat down, the table would be filled in no time flat. It wasn't anything she did. She was just friendly, smiling, and pretty; but the guys really liked her. As it turned out, she and I both married within a year of each other, and fortunately our husbands became friends, too.

One day we were carpooling to work together in her big yellow Buick. She was driving, and we had gotten about half-way to work when I realized I'd left my ID badge at home. So, rather than stop and get a temporary badge, we decided to turn around and go back to my house to pick up my badge. That made us late, so Barbara decided to push that old Buick on down the parkway a bit faster. It wasn't long until a policeman pulled us over, and she got a ticket for speeding. I felt so badly for her because it was my fault, and I did pay for the ticket. I think that was the last time I ever forgot my badge.

She and I sometimes attended gospel singings locally a few times just before we married, and I grew to love that genre of music more and more. I was already a Southern Gospel Music fan and went to singings with my sisters and mother. But I look back on all the good times Barbara and I shared, and realize how blessed I was to have her for a friend. I do recall it was she who introduced me to pizza. I had never had pizza until I was about 19 years old. So I always think of Barbara when I have pizza.

Other friends that have always been important to me from my youth are a couple or girls I met while going to college in Huntsville. Jimmie Sue, Mona, Jim's cousin Nancy and I was a gang of four that sometimes expanded to a gang of six or eight depending on what we decided to get into on a particular day.

Once we decided to take a ride with a fellow who had a car over to a place in Huntsville that they called the Honey Hole. Now, don't get upset with me for calling it that. It was not a name I gave it, but it was in the colored section of town. None of us girls had ever heard of it, and we'd never been there, but we were game to find out what it was and why it was called the Honey Hole.

I have to admit, I never found out why it was called that. It was just a neighborhood of rundown houses and the people were obviously poor. We didn't stay...just drove through so we could always say we'd been to The

Honey Hole. However, I don't think any of us ever did say we had. We probably were a bit ashamed of driving through looking at people who were worse off than us.

Another day, my friend Nancy and I decided to skip class and go to a movie. We did, and I have to be honest. Even though I enjoyed that movie, I was so uncomfortable skipping class that I promised myself I'd never do that again. I didn't. The class I skipped was taught by an older woman whose eyes pointed in different directions, and I never could tell if she was talking to me. I got in trouble more times than I care to admit because I didn't answer when she asked a question. It wasn't that I didn't know the answer. I couldn't tell if she was looking at me or someone else. Bless her heart, she meant well, I'm sure.

Since I came from a small town, and there were no public toilets in my small town, I had never really seen separate bathrooms for Whites and Blacks until I moved to Huntsville in 1956. Or at least, I don't recall seeing any. Yes, that was before the civil rights movement, and in the South Blacks (or colored as they were called then) had separate water fountains and bathrooms. I remember when we'd hang out around the courthouse in Huntsville going to the bathroom marked White and using the fountain marked White. I would see the Blacks going into separate facilities, but didn't think a lot about it. It was just the way things were back then. Not that meant they were right.

I did not go to school with Blacks because our schools were separate, and I didn't know anything different. But today I realize that Blacks had as much right as any of us and should not have been separated. I'm glad that they now have equal rights as the rest of the population, and I hope that we never go back to those days. I am not prejudiced, and I don't want anyone suffering because of being singled out. With that being said, however, I think our government needs to be more careful about allowing people to come into our country who only wish to terrorize us and cause our government to fail. I am prejudiced against terrorism in any form regardless of who the perpetrators are.

I'm thankful for our Constitution, our Bill of Rights and those men who had the knowledge, no doubt God given knowledge, to establish our government. We have a beautiful country, a unique country. I hope none of us ever forget to give thanks to the Lord for his bountiful goodness in placing us here at this time and place.

Foods of the South

Churning Butter... When I was a kid, I often had to make butter by using a churn. Today, you walk into the store and purchase your butter in a nice one pound package that has been divided into half-cup portions. We didn't have access to the factory produced butter. You made your own, especially in the World War II era.

First you had to have a 4-5 gallon stone churn with a wooden lid and dasher. Every house I ever visited in my younger days had one of these standing in the kitchen.

To this large stone jar, you filled it about half full or slightly over, with rich milk that contained a lot of cream. Then it was left to "turn" or "clabber." Depending on the temperature this could take a while or not so long. It seemed as if we filled the churn one night and it would be ready the next afternoon, but I am sure this was in the summertime. It probably took longer in the winter.

To test the readiness of the milk after it has clabbered, Mama would tilt the churn slightly and if the milk was just right for churning, she would put me to work. I knew that milk that had "blinked" or turned sour was not good for churning, and I'd always hope that had happened. It didn't. Mama had eagle eyes and knew what she was doing in the kitchen.

To churn the milk, I had to lift the dasher up and down, up and down, for what seemed like hours until the butter formed. In reality, it was probably only about 30-45 minutes that I had to sit at the churn and lift that dasher up and down, but it seemed forever to a child. Repetitive work has never been my forte.

Since the temperature has to be just right for the butter to form, Mama would periodically check the formation of the butter. If the butter didn't stick together, it showed that the milk was too cold and needed a bit of hot water added, and if it had a foamy appearance, she knew it needed the addition of a bit of cold water.

When I had dashed away long enough, Mama would take over the butter making process. She would remove the lid and stir the butter with the dasher to bring it together. Then she'd life it out of the churn, drain the butter, and place it in a bowl. I've seen her "work" the soft butter a bit to rid it of the milk, and then she would add a bit of salt and place it in a butter mold in the refrigerator. The butter mold had a press so that excess water could be squeezed out and the butter released from the mold when it was cold.

Mama used the butter for cooking and serving at the table. Strangely enough, as a child I did not like butter on toast or biscuits, so I seldom ate it. In fact, it wasn't until I hit my middle years that I learned to appreciate butter on a hot biscuit or potato. No doubt I missed a lot of good country cooking by being such a finicky eater.

Today most people know little or nothing about the process of making butter since it comes neatly packaged at the grocery store. But to be honest, the old homemade butter is some of the best you'll ever eat since it is sweet and fresh. Besides the left over milk was what was tasty to me – buttermilk when it is cold has a taste I prefer over "sweet" milk.

Hog Killing Time...I can remember people saying, "It's cold enough to kill hogs." I knew what that expression meant because I was around before slaughter houses and supermarkets were in our part of the world. The saying meant that the weather was really, really cold, and down South that means somewhere below 32 degrees—probably even in the 20s, but I'm not certain.

I do remember when it got cold enough to kill hogs. I never saw a hog slaughtered, only after it had been dissected and was being cut into appropriate means of safekeeping. The last hog killing that is vivid in my mind had to have been in the early 1940s. It was a very cold day when Daddy and some of the men helping him brought the slaughtered hog home and spread it out on tables in the back yard to butcher into hams, shoulders, loins, backbones, and meat for sausages and bacon. I remember thinking it was somewhat gross looking at those pieces that no longer resembled one of the hogs in our hog sty. All the hair had been removed along with all the innards, and it was ready for the more delicate work.

Mama always ground a lot of meat for sausages, and she knew how to season the meat with sage, salt and pepper and maybe other things that I wasn't aware of, too. I was usually assigned the job of helping making sausage patties for frying and then canning for the winter months. She also stitched cloth bags to place the mixture in so that they could be hung in the cooler months in the outbuilding to cure. My favorite was always the sausages that had been canned because they always tasted so fresh. I wasn't crazy about cooking the meat, but I did enjoy the sausage along with some of her homemade biscuits, but never at breakfast. I wasn't and still am not a breakfast person.

Hams and shoulders were always salted down and placed in wooden boxes to keep out rodents and bugs. The salt did the curing by bringing out the moisture. After a time, the hams and shoulders would also be hung to finish curing. Don't ask me how long that took. I don't know. I just know it was a time consuming process.

There is nothing like a good cured ham, sugar or salt cured. It has a flavor that a fresh ham is totally missing, and if it is cooked properly, it is like manna from heaven. If you ever purchase cured ham in a restaurant and it is tough as shoe leather, you know the chef did not know how to cook cured ham. I only know the way I cook cured ham, and that may not be appropriate way, but it suits me. I quickly cook it on each side, browning it enough to provide for some good gravy—redeye if that is the way you prefer it or just regular grave made from the pan scrapings, which is my preferred way. For the uninitiated, redeye gravy is made from the pan drippings where you cook the ham. You simply add about a half cup of water or coffee to the pan, stirring to loosen the juices that have cooked out of the ham, and cook for a couple of minutes. This is what you pour over the ham, grits, biscuits or whatever you like. It isn't my favorite gravy, but I have eaten it.

Farmers always helped one another at hog killing time, and our neighbors always turned out for ours. One thing farmers did not like was for the weather to turn too warm while the hams were curing. If flies were able to get into the building, they would lay eggs that formed an insect that no one wanted to dwell in their hams and shoulders. If a ham or shoulder was "blowed," the farmer would simply remove it from its hanger and carve out the area the flies had gotten to, rehang it and go on about their business. If I ever knew a piece of meat went through that process, I would refuse to eat meat until I was sure it was gone. I'm certain I missed out on a lot of good ham and shoulder meat by doing that, but I have always wanted my food to be as clean as possible, and that didn't include larva made from fly eggs. To me nothing could be more sickening. I would have thrown up had I been forced to eat it.

Making Souse or Head Cheese...I must insert a disclaimer at the very beginning of this section. I've never eaten Souse, but I did taste it once. It didn't taste bad, in fact, it smelled and tasted pretty good, but I just didn't like the greasiness of it. So I would not eat it. It was made from a hog's head, and that was enough reason for me to avoid it. However, most country people where I grew up used all the available meat from a hog, and the hog's head was part of the hog. It was clean. It was well prepared, but it did not appeal to me.

My mother was pretty particular about what she used to make souse, so she never used the entire head. She only used the jowls which had been previously thoroughly cleaned. She still soaked the jowls until the water ran clear, then she put them in a pot of clean water that she salted and cooked them slowly until the meat was very tender and fell apart.

When the meat was well done, she would put it through a meat grinder and add sage, red pepper, salt and black pepper to taste. She mixed all these seasonings thoroughly and then placed it in a mold and refrigerated it. I remember that the mold always had something heavy on top to squeeze it down into a solid mass for slicing.

I think Mama might have been the only one in the family who ate souse, but she did love it. She put a lot of pepper in it, and perhaps that is one reason only she ate it, though my brother Clay might have since he loved hot foods as a kid. It always smelled wonderful, but I just couldn't get past the greasiness of it because it did have cooked fat in it as well as the lean meat.

Souse or head cheese as some call it has pretty much faded into obscurity, but there may be a few of the older folks left in the world that enjoy this savory dish.

Miscellaneous Hog Parts...I've never eaten the miscellaneous parts of a pig. As my youngest sister Faye says, "If God intended us to eat liver, brains, tongue, lungs (lights), or hearts, he would have put them on the outside." I agree. That being said, I'm sure if any of us were really hungry enough, we might be willing to sample the inside of a hog, but until then I'm going to stay away from these gourmet items.

I can't even imagine eating the tongue of any animal, but if you have a hankering to try it, you need to know how to prepare it for cooking. First you pour boiling water over it and scrape the tongue to get rid of anything that has collected on the surface. (That's enough to stop me right there.) Then you boil it until it is tender seasoning with salt and pepper. Slice it and serve it warm with your side dishes. I read somewhere that people remove the outer skin before cooking it. That might help me get it past my nose, but I seriously doubt it.

A lot of people eat brains, but to be honest, I can't stand the sight of them and figure one brain per person is enough, and I still have mine. If you're buying them from a grocery store, you don't have to remove the thin veil that covers them, but if you're slaughtering your own, then you must. Most people I knew would cook them in a little water, adding salt and pepper, then when done, mash them with a potato masher and put them in a pan and scramble them with eggs. Sounds gross to me, but enjoy if you like.

Liver is one food I've never enjoyed. I simply can't get it past my nose. When I was in the hospital after having lost my first little boy in 1961, the hospital sent up liver for my dinner one day. My husband tried to convince me it was steak, but I knew it wasn't. He loved liver, so I gave him that "steak" and ate only the vegetables served with it. I still don't like liver, but I did learn to cook it for him and a neighbor of ours who lived on Darlene Circle in Huntsville years ago. They enjoyed it immensely, but I and the other wife, had steak instead.

Anyway most people know how to prepare and fry liver, so I won't go into details here, but I found that by frying a lot of onions when I made the liver, that I could tolerate being in the kitchen with it.

I simply cannot consider eating hearts or lungs (lights), but many people do. I remember hearing about people eating these two organs, but I never saw anyone cook them or prepare them. So if you want to know how to do it, you're going to have to ask some chef in a gourmet restaurant or travel to South America. They may still use those parts.

Some eat the stomach, but again I've never known or seen anyone eating stomach meat. Again, I'll say I already have a stomach, and I don't need another one inside or out. I think the thing that really makes me want to up-chuck is the idea of eating a pig's intestines. Chitterlings or "chittlins" are a delicacy in the South, and you have people who love them and people, like me, who can't conceive of putting something like that in their mouths. Chittlins are cut into sections, placed in a container of salt water and allowed to sit for three to four days. Then they are removed, rinsed, washed and rinsed again. When ready for cooking, they are cut into small pieces and the lining is removed. They are dipped into a batter made of flour, water, egg and baking powder and deep fat fried. Some prefer to roll them in corn mean and fry them. I've seen chittlins, but I've never tasted them, and I hope I never get hungry enough to have to eat them. I can't even imagine eating intestines of a hog, a cow or any other animal, but to those who do...enjoy!

As to the outer parts of the pig or cow, I have eaten ribs and nothing is more delicious than gnawing the meet off a barbequed rib. I've also eaten pig skins that have been fried crisp, but only the kind that comes in a package at the store. I've never made them myself. My mother did bake pork rinds during the depression and war years, and I have eaten some of those that were extra crispy. Daddy always said that his family ate everything but the squeal of the pig. If you're hungry enough, I'm sure you would. Most of us, however, prefer the hams, loins, shoulders and ribs of an animal. Now that is good eating.

Of course, there are pickled pigs feet, tail sections, fat that is rendered for later use, but you'll have to search the internet for secrets on how to use these items. Except for the fat, which is lard, I haven't had any experience with them.

Killing Chickens... As I've mentioned before, we grew all of our own vegetables and animals when I was a young child. We had chickens running around everywhere, and I, who was always running barefoot, was often angry when I stepped into chicken droppings and had to wash my feet. That would stop me from going barefoot for a while, but I loved the feel of the grass and warm dirt under my feet and Mama had a hard time keeping me in shoes. Country kids all were kind of Huck Finn types, and we enjoyed the lack of restraints in our daily lives. No matter how much our parents tried to teach us manners and how we were to act, we loved being "free range" kids. If you know what free range means when it comes to chickens today, then you know what I mean when I use that in terms of growing up. It was Mayberry before there was a Mayberry on TV. It was such a carefree existence. We were free to play in the creek, climb trees in the woods or in our orchard, hunt for crawdads, and eat our lunch under the shade tree if we wished. Everything was natural and organic. That's what I mean by being a free range kid, just as our chickens were free-range chickens. The chickens roamed and ate bugs and seeds, as well as being fed from feed that we kept for them. They laid eggs, and we ate some. Others were saved for hatching. When a hen got older and didn't lay eggs as often, she often made the ultimate sacrifice of being our Sunday dinner. Unlike kids today, we didn't get attached to the chickens as pets. We knew they were raised for their eggs and the meat they would put on the table, so we saved our petting for the family dog. Fortunately, we never ate dog meat, so the dogs were safe.

I remember watching Mama kill a hen for Sunday dinner. She knew her chickens well, and she knew the one that must make the sacrifice. Having been brought up on a farm, she also knew how to snap the neck on a chicken before hacking off the head and feet. She did this without flinching. It was expected of her, and she did what was necessary to fill our bellies.

Even after the old chicken was dead, it would flop around on the ground after losing its head quickly after the neck snapping, and that allowed some of the blood to flow out of the body, I'm guessing. Remember I was a small child when I remember seeing this done. I don't think I ever worried about it, but it might have been one thing that kept me in line when my Mama told me to behave.

Anyway, once the chicken quit flopping around (like a chicken with its head cut off if you remember the old saying), she would dip it in a pot of boiling water to loosen the feathers. Then picking off the feathers became the job of whichever of us kids happened to be around.

Once the feathers were off, the chicken was rinsed again and then cut open to expose the innards. Once the choice pieces were saved such as the liver and gizzard, it was then washed again and cut into pieces for frying. After that it was placed in the refrigerator and chilled. At some point, Mama would soak it in buttermilk before it was floured and fried.

I can still remember the smell of the chicken being fried on Sunday morning, and how eager I was to get home to that chicken for Sunday dinner.

Most people cannot relate to what I'm writing now because the generation after me grew up purchasing chickens from the supermarket and even later generations purchase theirs in boxes from KFC or from the freezer section of the supermarket in the form of frozen dinners. Ah…you've missed so much, you later generations, by having to eat chicken that has been mass produced, mass slaughtered and mass frozen or cooked. There is nothing quite as tasty as a good piece of chicken fresh from the farm…unless it is a fresh ear of corn from the garden.

The days when people grew their own food is almost gone. Small farmers have been taken over by subdivisions followed by strip malls. The way of life I once knew has fallen into history where it shall remain. Some of that is probably for the best, but unfortunately, it also leaves us totally vulnerable to whims of the markets and the powers that be.

I would not wish anyone to have to slaughter their own animals nor grow gardens as large as we once did because it is hard work. However, I think we'd all be better off if we did have to work a bit harder for our food. We might not be as overweight for one thing or suffer from many diseases that are related to our eating habits. Another benefit, no one needed a gym membership when I was a kid and before. I never knew anyone who was really overweight, except for a couple of slug bugs who didn't move around enough to keep their weight down. Most of us were slender, toned and had excellent natural suntans. There is something to be said for working for your food.

Ava's Southern Style Chicken Stew*

Ingredients:

2 pounds chicken breasts and thighs (if boneless use 1.5 pounds)
1 8-oz can tomato sauce
1 large onion chopped
1 can whole kernel corn (I use a cup of frozen)
salt, black & red pepper to taste
16 oz chopped or diced tomatoes w/pepper and celery
4 medium potatoes peeled and diced
1 tsp Tabasco Sauce (more if you like it spicy)
1 quart chicken broth
1 quart water
1 can cream style corn (add this about 10 minutes before serving. It helps to thicken the stew. It will burn if you add it with the other ingredients.

Place chicken parts in water and cook until meat is tender and falls off the bone. Remove from heat, pour off brother and save. Remove meat from bones and chop or shred (I shred). Place meat and one quart chicken brother into a large pot. Add all the ingredients except creamed style corn. Cook for approximately 40 minutes. Add the corn and heat for 10 minutes and serve.

Serve with hot cornbread or corn muffins. If not available, then soda crackers will do.

This makes a big pot of stew, and it is great the next day because the flavors blend even more after sitting overnight.

*This recipe came from a childhood friend in my hometown, Ava Hasting Haney. She was a good cook and made some of the best Chicken Stew I've ever eaten.

Now make some cornbread in a big iron skillet to go with it, invite some friends to share, and you've got a delicious Southern meal.

I should note that when I lived almost 22 years in Limestone County, AL that there was one guy who was known throughout the county for his chicken stew. That was Boss Hill. Yes, Boss was his real name. He was a wonderful old, southern gentleman who once each year in May, would set up cauldrons on his farm between Ardmore and Elkmont and cook up several huge pots of chicken and goat stew. He always had plenty, and it became a gathering place for all the politicians in the county to congregate and shake hands with the voters as well as enjoy Boss's stew. Boss often drove a horse and buggy in parades in the area, all the kids loved to see his outfit. He was a gentle, kind man, as was his lovely wife. I missed them when death took them from the community. There simply won't be another Boss Hill.

Cornbread Dressing

Ingredients:

4-5 cups crumbled cornbread – bake the day ahead for best results

3 or 4 pieces of "light" bread or biscuit, crumbled

2 cans *Swanson* chicken broth (13-3/4 ounce)

1 large onion, chopped

3 stalks celery, chopped

3 eggs – boiled and chopped

1/2 cup butter, melted or as desired

1 T Sage – or to taste

In a large bowl combine the cornbread and chicken broth, and allow this to sit for a while. Add the onions, celery, and eggs, mixing thoroughly. Add the melted butter. Place the mixture in a 9 x 13-inch baking pan. Bake in a 350-degree oven for 1 hour or until lightly browned on top and around the edges.

Bean Soup

Ingredients:

3 cups Great Northern Beans (or beans of choice) precooked
2 ham hocks or 2 slices of chopped ham
1 cup diced onions
1 cup diced celery
1 cup chicken broth
Water as needed to thin the soup

Cook the beans with the ham hock in enough water to keep them covered. Remember the beans will expand and soak up the water as they cook. If you want faster cooking beans, soak them overnight.

When the beans are almost done, add the onions, celery and chicken broth or water,
as needed, to thin down to a medium thick soup. Serve with cornbread

Sweet Potato Casserole

Ingredients:

5 sweet potatoes or yams
2 cups milk
½ tsp. Cinnamon
1 tsp. salt
¼ tsp. Allspice
¼ tsp. Nutmeg
½ stick butter
1 cup brown sugar

Peel the sweet potatoes and slice in about ¾ inch slices. Mix the potatoes with all the spices, sugar and milk and place in a casserole dish. Dot with butter. If the potatoes seem a bit dry, a small amount of water may be added to help them stay moist. Bake for approximately 45-50 minutes.

FYI: There is a lot of difference between a yam and a sweet potato. Both are good, and you can pretty much use them interchangeably in recipes, but yams are best in my estimation. They are usually darker and somewhat sweeter.

Mama's Fried Apples

Ingredients:

5 or 6 Yellow Delicious apples, cored and sliced – or use apples of your choice. Do not peel.
½ cup water
About 4 Tbsp butter
1/2 cup sugar (more or less)

In a large cast iron skillet, place water in pan, melt the butter on medium heat, then place the apples in the pan and cook until almost done. This should take about 15 minutes, but might take longer. You can tell when the apples begin to change color. Then add the sugar (more if you're using tart apples) and "fry", turning from time to time, until the sugar has melted and has formed a nice syrupy juice in the pan. Don't walk away from your apples for long at a time. They need stirring to keep from burning. If your apples aren't juicy, you may need to add a tiny bit of water to help them form a syrup.

Serve the apples as a side dish, but they are good served over vanilla ice cream for dessert. A bit of cinnamon is also good, but not traditional.

Caramel Pie

Ingredients:

1 cup sugar (brown in hot skillet, stirring constantly until a caramel color)
2 cups milk
4 eggs, separate yolks and whites, beaten
3 Tbsp flour
1 tsp vanilla
½ tsp Cream of Tarter

Filling: In a double boiler or a very heavy pan, cook milk, beaten egg yolks and flour until thick.
When thick, add the mixture to the brown sugar, stirring to mix. Add the vanilla and pour into a baked pie shell.

Meringue: Beat the four egg whites which have come to room temperature with 4 T. sugar and Cream of Tartar until they hold soft peaks (don't over beat). Spoon meringue over pie filling and place the pie in a 300 degree F. oven to lightly cook and brown. This doesn't take long, so keep an eye on them. Meringue burns very fast, so don't walk away and leave it.

If you're Southern born, you probably ate pralines from the time you were able to chew. This southern has a creamy texture . It may take you a couple of tries before getting it just right, but when you do, you'll want to try them again and again.

Pralines

Ingredients:
2 cups sugar
¾ tsp soda
1 cup light cream

Mix these ingredients well and stir carefully to keep from getting sugar crystals on the side of the pan. Bring to a boil, stirring occasionally to prevent the mix from burning. When it starts to bubble high, reduce the heat and continuing stirring. Cook to a soft ball stage using a candy thermometer or the less accurate old fashioned way of dropping a small amount of the syrup in a cup of water. If it forms into a soft ball you are at the correct stage.

Remove from the heat and add the following ingredients:
1.5 T butter...be sure to only add that much butter or the pralines will not harden, and 2 cups of pecan halves.

Beat this mixture until it thickens enough to drop by spoon. Drop each spoonful on waxed paper or on the new non-stick foil that is on the market and allow to

Grits, Country Ham and Red Eye Gravy

If there is one thing that distinguishes the South from other parts of the country, it is hominy grits, country ham and red-eye gravy. Other areas may serve grits, but it mostly below the Mason/Dixon Line that you'll find the combination of grits, country ham and red-eye gravy served. In today's modern world, chefs have discovered grits, and they cook them in all sorts of ways adding cheese, kale, broccoli, shrimp and perhaps the kitchen sink, but a purist knows that grits were made to go with country ham and red-eye grave. Here is a recipe of sorts. To be honest, you really almost have to be a Southerner to put this dish together, but if you're adventurous give it a try.

Grits:
1 cup grits cooked according to instructions on the package. Make sure you stir the grits to keep them from forming lumps.
Add butter, salt and pepper, to taste – set aside

Country Ham:
4 palm-sized pieces of country ham – about 3 ounces each
Enough oil in the pan to fry the ham.
A cast iron skillet…required!

Country ham is cured. So cook this ham on medium-high heat on each side…just enough to slightly brown the mean but not so long as to make it dry and tough to chew—no more than 5 minutes. Since I'm not a heavy salt eater, I like to rinse the salt cured country ham then pat it dry with paper towels before cooking. Once cooked, remove from pan and set aside while you prepare the red-eye gravy.

Red-Eye Gravy
½ cup water
1-2 T coffee to taste

In the ham the pan was cooked, leave all the drippings in the pan and add about ½ cup water to the pan and stir with a wooden spoon until all the meat tidbits are loosened, then stir in 1- 2 T of brewed coffee to the hot pan. Simmer until the gravy reduces to about a quarter of a cup. To plate, place the grits on a plate, add ham and pour redeye gravy over the ham and grits. Serve with eggs and biscuits.

Southern Style Banana Pudding

¾ cup sugar
Dash of salt
3 egg yolks, beaten
½ tsp. vanilla extract
2 cups milk
3 T flour

2-4 bananas, sliced
vanilla wafers
3 egg whites
6 T sugar

½ tsp. vanilla

Combine sugar, salt and flour, add to egg yolks and vanilla. Heat milk in a medium sized saucepan, slowly add the egg and sugar mixture. Cook on medium heat, stirring often to avoid sticking, until the sauce has thickened.

Arrange layers of vanilla wafers in the bottom and up along the sides of a shallow 1 ½ quart baking dish. Top the wafers with a layer of bananas add another layer of wafers and continue until the bowl is about filled. Top with the pudding mixture above.

For the Meringue, beat the room temp egg whites with the sugar and vanilla until stiff. Spread over the banana pudding and bake at 400 F until golden brown. (Keep an eye on it to keep it from burning). Serve warm or cold.

This pudding is best eaten on the first day, but it will hold overnight if necessary. If you don't like bananas, you can substitute canned pineapple chunks for the bananas in this recipe. Just make sure you drain them well.

Old Fashioned Southern Teacakes

2 ½ cups plain flour, sifted   ½ cup butter or shortening
¼ tsp salt   1 cup sugar
2 tsp baking powder   2 eggs, beaten
1 T milk   ½ tsp vanilla

Sift flour, salt and baking powder together. If using self-rising flour do not add salt or baking powder. Cream butter, sugar and eggs. Add vanilla and milk and mix thoroughly. Then add the flour and mix well. Place dough on a lightly floured board; sprinkle a little flour over the dough to keep it from sticking to the rolling pin, and roll ½ inch think. Cut with a biscuit cutter. Place on a cookie sheet and bake for 350 to 375 degrees for 12 to 15 minutes.

Your teacakes should be nice and soft and lightly browned. Wonderful when served warm with a cup of coffee or tea or a glass of milk.

Teacakes used to be found in almost all Southern cook's kitchen, but they have been pushed aside for commercial cookies. If your own grandmother has a recipe, try them!

This is one thing I can well remember my Granny Merrell always having handy at her house. I never visited her without getting a couple of big, fat teacakes.

Southern Fried Chicken

Chicken pieces (your choice)   Self-rising flour
Buttermilk   Salt and Pepper
Oil for frying

Remove skin from chicken (or leave on if you like crispy skin), then soak the chicken in buttermilk overnight. Next day place flour, salt and pepper in a paper or plastic bag and shake the chicken pieces in this until well coated. Heat a heavy skillet (preferably a cast iron skillet or Dutch oven) to medium high heat until it is quite hot, then lower the heat to about medium and drop the chicken into the pan with tongs so the grease doesn't splatter on you. Do not move the chicken until it is nicely browned on the first side, then flip and continue cooking until it is completely done. The cooking time will vary. The thicker the chicken the longer it will take to cook, and if it has bones in, that will also add to the time. To check, slice one of the thicken pieces and check for doneness. Do not cover, and do not crowd the pan.

If you want gravy to serve with rice or potatoes, leave just enough grease and any pieces of crust that may have flakes off in the pan, slowly stir in a little flour (about 1 T per 1 T of fat) and stir until slightly browned. Then stir in water or milk, your preference, and cook until thickened. Add liquid until it is the proper consistency. Salt and pepper before serving.

Lemon Fluff

(or Sawdust and Calf Slobbers)

Filling

1 14oz can evaporated milk
1 sm pkg lemon Jello
1 cup sugar

¼ cup lemon juice
1 ¾ cups hot water

Crust

16 graham crackers crushed
¼ cup sugar

1/3 cup margarine

Mix these 3 ingredients and line the bottom of a 9x13 inch pan.

Chill unopened can of milk. Mix Jello and hot water. Chill until partially set. Whip Jello and water until foamy and fluffy. Add lemon juice and sugar . Whip chilled evaporated milk and fold into Jello mixture. Use care in folding so you don't release all the air you've just whipped into the mixtures.

Line the bottom of a 9x13 inch pan with graham cracker crust and pour mixture into pan. Chill until set.

At Blanche High School, we had some wonderful cooks. I don't remember all their names, so I won't even try to do so here, but I do remember that our hot lunches were wonderful. Not only was there lots of good food for hungry kids, but the cooks were always so nice to each of us. I honestly don't know how they could be with such a hungry horde acting up and shoving each other around in line, but they were wonderful. I still remember the delicious Lemon Fluff dessert they made for us, so I've included a receipt here. It is very similar to the dessert we called Sawdust and Calf Slobbers...something that farm kids would know about. The closest recipe I've found for this dessert is one given to me by a sweet friend in Overland Park, KS, Susan Ninstil. She isn't from the South though she has lived in Florida. Anyway, I hope you'll make this dessert and think of those wonderful lunchroom ladies.

I realize there are some in other parts of the country who think Paula Deen, bless her heart, is the epitome of a Southern cook. Now I like to watch Paula and her sons, and she is good. But I've never known anyone where I grew up that used so much butter. We do like to fry foods, and we do like to season well, but there are a lot of ways to season food without using so much butter. I've tried to explain to people that if you travel from one side of the South to the other, you'll not only find different dialects and accents but also different ways of cooking. Paula and Emeril Lagasse have both become famous for different types of Southern foods, but they have only written part of the book on Southern cooking. Ask any Southern cook who watched her mother or grandmother cook, and she'll tell you she learned from them—usually without the use of a written recipe. We have very different cuisines in various parts of the South. I enjoy the dishes that are native to various areas, such as Kentucky Burgoo, Brunswick stew, tiny Gulf Coast shrimp, Chesapeake oysters, and Tennessee Valley BBQ, and I'm thankful that the South is so diverse. If you're driving through the South on vacation, you can expect to find foods prepared along the coast are different from those prepared by inland cooks. Sample and enjoy them all. There are many good cooks in the South.

Southern Expressions

Below are a few Southern expressions. I know most that live in the South know these and use them regularly, but for those new to the area, I'm including a few so that they can join in the conversation at the local cafes and bars.

- She will argue with a sign post and paint it herself. (argumentative)
- He ain't right upstairs. (crazy)
- She looks like she's been rode hard and put up wet (exhausted).
- That is about as useful as a sidesaddle on a pig. (useless)
- It's hot enough to fry eggs on the pavement. (very hot)
- He is so stuck up that if it rains, he'll drown with his nose so high in the air. (arrogant)
- He's so full of it that his eyes have turned brown. (You can guess what the it is.) (lying)
- She's got about as much sense as a goose. (nutty)
- He's a lying, low down skunk. (about as bad as one can be)
- If I tell you it's gonna rain, grab your umbrella. (trust me)
- He's dumber than a rock. (IQ of 30)
- I have to go to the bathroom before my eyes float.
- I'm sweating harder than a prostitute going to meeting (sinner going to a revival)
- She's madder than an old wet hen. (don't mess with her or else)
- You ain't whistling Dixie. (You're being honest)

   This saying originated during the Civil War when Yankee soldiers would whistle the song Dixie when they thought they were near Confederate soldiers to make the Rebels think they were Confederate soldiers. Therefore, if you tell the truth, you aren't whistling Dixie.

- I'm so tired of hearing you two fuss and fight, I'm going to tie your tails together and toss you over the clothesline. (like two cats fighting).
- He's just an old coot. (odd, eccentric or stubborn).
- You're dumb as an ox. (no explanation needed for this).
- If wishes were horses, pigs would fly. (impossible dreams)
- He/she can't carry a tune in the bucket. (sings off key)
- I'll smack you so hard, you'll see tomorrow. (a nice wallop)
- Well, I'll swaney! (used as a mild, and possibly more ladylike swear word).
- No don't go off half cocked. (be ready)
- I'm fixing to put on more clothes (no, it is not additional clothing...it means different clothing.
- If you don't stop whining I'll give you something to whine about.
- Don't count your chickens before they hatch. (don't count on it).
- You're barking up the wrong tree. (you're wrong)
- You need to fish or cut bait. (get on with what you are doing)
- I got the short end of the stick (I lost that battle, argument or got the losing end of it).
- Well, hold your horses. (be patient)
- Stop being a worry wart (stop fretting over something you can't control).
- She's a feisty filly. (spirited girl)
- He's like a bump on a log (lazy, do nothing, loafer)

A word of caution: If you are not a native-born Southerner or haven't lived in the South the major portion of your life, please don't try to mimic our drawl or accent. You just can't do it no matter how hard you try. You will always sound like a fake, just as they do on TV and in movies when they try to make fun of the South and our drawl.

Addendum

Since this book was first printed, I have gone back through and corrected some typos and clarified a couple of things that got lost in the process. I've also added a table of contents.

I have so many more stories to tell that I wish I had included in this book, but I will leave those for another time. For all of you who have already purchased this book, I want to say thank you.

If you enjoyed this book, please go to Amazon.com and give me a review.

Loretta Merrell Ekis

Contact: lekis@kc.rr.com

May the road rise up to meet you.
May the wind be always at your back.
May the sun shine warm upon your face;
the rains fall soft upon your fields
and until we meet again,
may God hold you in the palm of His hand.

(A traditional Gaelic blessing)

Made in the USA
Charleston, SC
20 September 2013